SleepingFish 8

SleepingFish 8

ISBN (13): 978-0-9798080-9-8
ISBN (10): 0-9798080-9-X

Edited by Gary Lutz and Derek White

Cover art by Eduardo Recife
designed by Derek White

For more information and additional online works, see

<www.sleepingfish.net>

Published by Calamari Press, New York, NY

<www.calamaripress.com>

Contents

Stephen Hastings-King	5	*Imagination Factory & Burning Words*
Ryan Call	10	*The Tornadic Life Cycle*
Anna DeForest	12	*The Lemon Wife*
Sasha Fletcher	14	*when you get swallowed by the sidewalk chances are if you don't die you will ...*
Nina Shope	19	*The Rooms*
Rachel May	21	*Good.*
David McLendon	25	*Provenance*
Eugene Lim	26	*The Parable of Our Giant*
The Brothers Goat	27	*The Study & The Spot*
Lito Elio Porto	31	two from *A Dictionary of Hues*
Adam Weinstein	35	*Slicing Nails*
Diane Williams	39	*Carnegie Nail*
Dennis Cooper	40	*The Lonesome Deaths of Bud and Sandy*
Elliott Stevens	41	*The Men from Life*
Tim Jones-Yelvington	44	*Bathhouse in 5 Senses*
Alec Niedenthal	45	*And Given the Chance to Be Safe*
Amelia Gray	50	*The Vanished*
Matt Bell	53	*Abelard, Abraham, Absalom & Isaac, Isaiah, Ishmael*
Eduardo Recife	55	two images from *Collage Book*
David Ohle	57	excerpt from *The Camp*
Evelyn Hampton	62	*About the Inside*
Émilie Notéris (tr. by Laure Motet & Monica Karski)	67	*Moleskin*[Weapon]
Ottessa Moshfegh	73	*Dakota*
Cooper Renner	79	The Introduction to *Christabel: a Fiction*
Christine Schutt	85	*An Invitation & Blank*
M. T. Fallon	88	from *An Introduction to the Work of Ivan Menchov* by Igor Lenchov
Daniel Grandbois	93	*Thirteen Shapes, Tubes, The Switch, Maude & Instructions*
Julie Doxsee	97	*Lightning, Girls on the Run, Summary of a Moon Film & Blue Kill*
Terese Svoboda	101	*Dancing for Rain*
Blake Butler	103	*Blown Exits*
Stephen Gropp-Hess	107	*On Water and the City*
Ali Aktan Aşkın	114	*on funeral*

Imagination Factory

I sit in a small office amongst a huge pile of letters picking out individuals and arranging them on a big square made of something like paraffin. It is one of a series of small offices in which other selves sit amongst huge piles of letters picking out individuals to arrange on a big square made of something like paraffin.

We have to be careful where the letters are positioned and even more not to include too much: these are not stories but parameters of stories, the parameters people use to shape them. They have to come from somewhere.

When we are finished with a square, we make another in which each type of letter used becomes an element in a circle. Then we draw lines connecting them. We call them gates. There cannot be more than 261. Usually, the target number is much lower than that. The number of gates determines the range of permutations. The permutations are stories.

On the wall over my desk, like there is over every other such desk in this department, an advertising poster. It says:

> Twenty Six foundation letters.
> He engraved them, He carved them.
> He permuted them, He weighed them
> He transformed them,
> And with them He depicted all that was formed
> and all that would be formed.

Sometimes I think about him, the fictional craftsman we created as a public image that we later had to put out of business.

When someone finishes a square, they carefully carry it out of their office to another room in which there is a metal conveyor belt that carries them through a complex of ovens and laminating machines. The squares are melted and remolded around the letters, holding them together. They emerge at the far end of the conveyor system as transparent structures which are stacked on pallets. Forklifts move them to another area that I rarely visit. That area fashions and affixes to the back of these structures the fine, intricate gearing which enables them to fit into the appropriate area of cultural machinery.

I haven't traveled much further than my office since I started writing a text about Zeno that will not end. From the moment it arrived, I suspected it was a trap, a way for management to sideline me. I wracked my memory going through all the interactions with management I could recall, trying to find the moment I made a wrong move and gave offense. I couldn't think of one.

Orders arrive by tube from upstairs. They come in metal cynlinders that make a hollow sound when they arrive. There was a time when I got many work orders:

Short story template: boy meets girl, boy looses girl, boy gets tractor.

Constitution of small country. Rationale for the Office of President for Life.

Advertisement: how eating red sausages made of processed meat by-products makes life more worth living.

My tube has not sounded for a long time now. My work is always half-way finished. No matter what I do, it is always half-way finished.

We make templates. Forms they're called. What we do is important: without forms, no-one can dream anything, write anything, make anything.

We occupy a fundamental position in the way capitalism operates. We design imaginations.

Despite that, we are a shy company. Marketing prefers that products be thought of as platonic forms or as the products of some distant craftsman. The forms are for advertisements which emphasize something grand; the craftsman for ads that personalize. We are shy because we are not interested in brand identity: quite the opposite. We mass produce templates that allow people inside capitalism to dream. You know, to dream appropriate things. We are technicians of desire because we are technicians of expression. Inserting a brand between people and what they dream and desire would disrupt the circuits of dreaming and desire. Ours is the anti-brand.

Our business is recession-proof. No matter how bad things get, people want to dream. In order to dream, they have to have patterns. So day after day, we stamp them out.

The firm is very big: lots of departments. I work in the Northeast Sector, Writing Division.

But I digress.

Letters are produced by putting old letters into huge vats which are heated. This is a dangerous operation and happens in the basement. People wearing white uniforms and safety glasses monitor round glass gauges, sometimes turning valves to release ammonia god knows where it goes. Once in a great while something happens down there and a bell rings and we all go stand in the parking lot. In total silence we watch the fire department and emergency crews arrive. Everyone is nervous. Much is at stake in the continued production of imagination.

Burning Words

I remember words stacked beside a fireplace like logs. On the wall, there's a photograph of cords of them outside somewhere else visible through a window, presumably drying in the air.

I am being told how to start a fire with them.

Newspaper doesn't stay aflame long enough: use a Duraflame of Stupid.

I am talking with a marketing person. I am standing in a showroom.

I am told: They aren't actual stupidity, you know. We just call them that. It's an inside joke.

Have you ever thought about where they all go? Words I mean. After you use them. They seem to disappear into the air. But words are insects with very short lifespans. They are born, they develop very quickly, they mate through contact with other words, they lay eggs and then die. We were the first to figure this out.

We experimented with various uses for them because the supply is everywhere and grows very fast but if there are no uses there's no point in even remembering that they can be harvested. After many experiments, we found that words are flammable once they are dried and cured. So now we collect them, trying to be inefficient about it because there are so many. We dry them and then put them in the air to cure. Then sell them. For burning.

Not everyone is comfortable with using them because they confuse the dried words with ones that still carry complexes of association with them, but that's not right. Those complexes are produced by the electrical underpinning of the insect metabolisms. When they pass through, these electrical underpinnings interact with ours and together produce these phenomena which we transpose into our frames of reference using filters of our own.

We try to discourage people from playing with dried words. We say just think of them as a fuel source. You don't make structures out of logs of pine you're about the throw in the fire. But people see them and this starts more insects into their lifecycles. And this confuses them. We try to tell people that the words in your mind are different from the words that you're holding. That's just the way it is. But that is not easy for people to grasp.

When you buy dried words from us, you're buying words that have passed through as many cognitive spaces as there are words. They never were yours. If one by chance passed through your hands that started out in your environment, you wouldn't recognize it. We've done extensive tests on this.

So we have found that despite the fact that this is an endlessly renewal energy source the market for them is very limited. Words are a boutique item. So we opened these upscale little stores in select cities. Test marketing. Thanks for stopping by.

I say: But wait. How did you realize that words are insects?

I am told: Frames of reference are powerful. We only find what we're looking for. The last thing people imagine is that words are insects, but here we are. Think of it like time. For us, in general, there is time, a container world that we move through. We agree that there is this container world and on aspects of how we move through it. But what if this shared experience just leans on something about the cyclical features of the electrical systems that underpin how we operate? Electrical systems: that's what we are. So for us there is such a thing as time. But that doesn't mean that there is such a thing as time. There are whole worlds in what we are not looking for.

I say: But how exactly did you see that words are insects? And how did you figure out that these insects would burn if you dry them?

I am told: Company secrets, sir.
We're closing now.
Thanks for stopping by.

STEPHEN HASTINGS-KING lives next to a salt marsh in Essex Massachusetts where he makes constraints, works on prepared piano with the collectives Holiday in Spain and Clairaudient (www.clairaudient.org), and writes entertainments of various types.

The Tornadic Life Cycle

For the purposes of this field guide, we have divided the deceased farmer's 'tornadoing' into five easily discernable stages of the tornadic life cycle: *funnel cloud, tornado simple, mature tornado, shrinking tornado* and *decaying tornado.* While these classifications allow an informed and capable individual to engage in the identification of, escape from, and peaceful coexistence with the deceased farmer and his emotional whims, the North American public should understand that tornadoes, and the deceased farmers within them, have been known to engage in other, sometimes erratic behaviors, such as soil redistribution, incessant cattle driving, and the violent dispersal of illegal aliens. Therefore, we must ask that you remain alert to the possibility of a tornado's unpredictably deviating from the model below, especially if you suddenly find yourself without shelter, stumbling alone across the plains:

1) The rotating column of air, or *funnel cloud*, develops at altitude and marks the deceased farmer's descent from the lowest levels of the storm system. The *funnel cloud* is both a warning sign and a cautious display of affection, often visible to all individuals within a ten-mile radius. At this stage, the deceased farmer has yet to be reminded of his inability to achieve physical love, his loss of contact with old friends, the crowd of family members mourning over his grave.

2) When the *funnel cloud* makes contact with the ground, also known as 'kissing the earth,' by definition we have a *tornado simple.* It is during the *tornado simple* stage that the deceased farmer resorts to his old ways, which we have called 'harvesting.' This includes, but is not limited to, such farmstead activities as shucking corn, combine operation, posthole-digging, and the various tasks of general home repair. The deceased farmer's harvesting is, of course, an error of massive proportions, and sends the tornado on a devastating path throughout the countryside.

3) During the tornado's mature stage, the funnel reaches its greatest width, which may vary on a case-by-case basis as a result of the speed with which the deceased farmer 'harvests.' The *mature tornado* is almost always vertical and most of the time touches the ground, though skipping in especially unstable tornadoes does occur, depending upon

how distraught the deceased farmer becomes. The *mature tornado* causes severe damage to whatever it encounters, alive or otherwise, a result of the deceased famer's full-blown rage and desperation to live again.

4) While it is true that the *mature tornado* is most destructive, it is in fact the *shrinking tornado* that causes the greatest number of fatalities per year. Although we are uncertain as to why this is, various meteorologists have suggested that the deceased farmer's desire to revoke the privilege of life from those around him exponentially increases in direct proportion to the shrinking of the tornado, causing the farmer to lash out angrily in response to his weakening hold upon the earth. While we certainly understand and support this theory, we must also point out that the stupid, slow, and unskilled make up a vast percentage of the fatalities, suggesting, perhaps, that as the tornado shrinks, the doomed emerge prematurely from their shelters to investigate the damage, to take pictures, to film the storm in the hopes of sending video to the local news channel, unaware of the statistic that they will soon become.

5) Even the most paranormal of forces must respect the laws of entropy, and thus decay soon becomes the tornado: the emotional energy of the deceased farmer weakens, begins to dissipate; the *decaying tornado* writhes improbably above the landscape, its once solid funnel reduced to a thin, untwisting bit of rope; the disturbed earth settles anew, prepares to heal itself; and those men, women, and children left unscathed assemble brightly in the muddy fields to applaud the tornado's final moments, to send the deceased farmer skyward with hearty ceremony. Perhaps it is this act of reverence for the otherworldly that explains the continued appearance of tornadoes across our nation, for what kind of ghost would forsake the chance to reap one final time the benefits that accompany the cold offices of death?

RYAN CALL lives in Houston with his wife. Excerpts from his ongoing North American field guide to weather have been published by *mlpress* and *Lamination Colony*.

The Lemon Wife

Ever headed home from somewhere? A real shame when you get there. A few steps in, lift your head, really smell the air in there? And it smells awful, and it doesn't smell at all, and then you know you are not enough of an oozing, aching body to musk up even a box-bare rented room? So you take up smoking, you smoke for the smell, but then you cannot smell—not even smoke, specifically not smoke—because you smoke too much?

Ever get home from somewhere, from the drugstore, say, and take off your shoes and get in bed and stay there? Stay stiff and twitch, you feel like waiting, teeth-gritted visceral waiting, tense like for the phone to ring? But you do not own a phone, or if you do, you can never remember the number fast enough when it is asked for? You sequence the numbers wrong, you mix the ones and sevens, or you say—not even numbers—you say letters, you spell things, make words to assemble, but no one assembles the words you are making, and no one is listening, and no one even asked?

Ever love them anyway? Ever remember to love someone anyway? Ever love the woman at the drugstore, by the hand soap at the drugstore, and love her for touching with her short soft hands only the soaps with citrus scent? No vague citrus, either. Not even lemon straight, but lemon-lime or mandarin or lemon-melon-mint? You love how she touches the bottles, how she turns them in her short soft hands. Later in bed you pretend she is alone with you somewhere, that you share soap at a sink there, and you smell her hands after, and you smell your hands after, and it is the same smell, and you love her?

Ever wake and find her, still and tense, in the bed where you were pretending? Find that now it is her bed, find that now you are her husband, already you are husband to this hand-soap woman? And she has been your wife a while, and waiting in the bed a while, for you to do something aboard her? About her? You cannot figure what. And now she is angry, she has been waiting enough already, and she has been wedded enough already, and her hips are spreading now and messy, and you never want to smell her hands, and when you do, you smell them and smell nothing, you get nothing from them, you can smell nothing at all, because you smoke too much?

Ever wonder where the scent went so quickly? Wonder was it lost over time, in the end, all in one, at the start, at the drugstore? At the second you met the woman with the soap, learned her name and followed her along: to the birthmarks, the lapsing hygiene, the crippled way at writing cramped, left-handed notes she could not mean, notes that thank you for things you never did, full of names you cannot face and places no one has heard of?

What if, at the store that day, you had gamely passed? Surveyed her turning the citrus soap, studied the poise of her short soft hands? Maybe, in passing, you slipped the hard side of your hand barely by her skirt, just at the high hem, and skimmed—maybe, barely—the soft back of one bare leg? And if you had the need, if you really did need more, you could have circled the store until you saw which soap she settled on, and settled yourself the same. You could have had the secret, the same-smelling hands, but none of the rest, none of the wife—just the hard side, the soft leg, and hand soap to wash with alone.

Ever sleep alone? And then wake, and then see, so suddenly, how always, how altogether, how all throughout the whole of it you must have been alone, because you are still in bed—but your shoes are on? And you do not have an angry wife, a lemon wife, or any kind otherwise; you cannot be a husband, even, because you are not a man. A woman then! And enough already.

Ever smoke too much in bed, at ease while you do because your shoes are on? Almost as though, should you fall asleep smoking, and you must wake up to flee the fire, it will be all right—because the shoes? And while you smoke in bed you pretend it, you start to pray it, even, that you will fall asleep smoking, that the sheets will catch, that you will smell no smoke and the show will end then, will burn to the end then, shoes and all the rest?

Ever only learned you were asleep from waking, waking with your shoes on, alone and in ashes and maybe you should go somewhere? Just somewhere? Just go somewhere. Just go.

Anna DeForest is living in Brooklyn.

WHEN YOU GET SWALLOWED BY THE SIDEWALK CHANCES ARE IF YOU DON'T DIE YOU WILL END UP IN A SMALL HOUSE WITH A CHIMNEY

—Tell me about the house. About the time you spent underground. Wasn't there water in the floor of the house underground.
—Yes. Or. There was a waterfall and how it fell was through the kitchen

—Were there not fish in that
—All we ate were birds

—And where did you get the birds
—I pulled them from her

—And where did they come from before that
—What are you getting at?

—What do you think I am getting at
—It is none of my business where the birds come from
don't look to me for how things happen in this world

—I am certainly not looking to you for that
—Then what then.

—Why would someone hide a bird in their mouth
—Why would someone keep an ocean in their chest

—All fair questions
—Thank you

—You are welcome. So. The bird. When was the first time you'd seen it
—She saw it in a dream but I saw it on the roof. It was out a window. I didn't open the window.

—Why not?
—I don't know. I felt it would swallow me. I felt it would take me somewhere. I was not at that time ready to be taken.

—But these were just feelings
—They were valid feelings

—I am not saying that the feelings you feel are not valid
—Thank you

—I am not saying that at all. That would be rude.
—It wouldn't be polite

—But they were just feelings

Please tell me what happened.

I woke up because it was loud. When I woke up she was still asleep. How she was still asleep I did not understand. It must have been magic. Magic is the only reasonable explanation for this is what I thought. I went to the roof. I was hoping for her to get up soon. I myself have often left places I wasn't supposed to be when there was a loud sound like thunder clapping.

I wanted to take that sound and keep it in a drawer. I wanted to keep this drawer inside of my chest.

I was thinking about sleeping. I was thinking about leaving. About just getting up and going downstairs and getting a nice glass of water. I kept thinking about it until it was like I did it. Which was great.

I was thinking about being lonely. I was thinking about feeling lonely. I was thinking about worrying about loneliness. I was worrying about loneliness. I was worrying about worry. I was worried. I was worried the thunder would wake her up and she would not go back to sleep and she would be cranky and I would have to deal with that. I was thinking about how I could always walk away when things got hard but that didn't last very long because I would end up walking really far down the road and suddenly every house I walked into was mine and all my teeth were gathered on the walls all nailed up like a mouth and smiling.

I was worried there was something wrong with my mouth like it was full of dirt from sleeping in the ground. I had not been sleeping in the ground. I do not remember having slept in the ground. I woke her up and said Have I been sleeping in the ground and she said Yes now stop that and went back to sleep. I shook her awake again and I can't remember what happened after that but the room lit up briefly.

I was worried I could not fit the lightning back into my pocket and it would wander around for days on end.

I was worried the thunder wouldn't wake her and she would never wake up and we would never have sex again and no one would tell me when I was getting carried away.

The thunder hit so hard it set off every car alarm for blocks. I will stop all of this I said. I am getting so very tired. I climbed up on the roof. From there I went up into the sky.

Up in the sky there were clouds and it was loud. What were the clouds like? They were loud. There was thunder. There was lightning.

Up in the sky all I found were tin cans. One of them said Hey where did you go. The ground opened up and I fell into your arms.

I was underground and so were you. We slept in the dirt until it grew into a house for us. It was a very small house. There was one room. There may have been a bathroom or a waterfall. There was a waterfall. It fell through the floor. In it were all sorts of things.

She said I am hungry. I pulled birds out of her ears and we cooked them in a frying pan. This has got to stop she said. What are we doing underground she said.

When you get swallowed by the sidewalk chances are if you don't die you will end up in a small house with a chimney and no matter what you do the chimney will not be able to get you home.

How do you know the chimney will not get us home she said. I said because I am not Dick Van Dyke and you are not Mary Poppins and neither of us have any umbrellas.

I grew us a garden in the dirt under the ground. Look I said I am making things without paper. I don't believe you she said. All sorts of things passed between us. She came out to the garden while I slept and fixed it I think. I think that is what was happening. But I was asleep.

How are we going to get home she said. What do you mean I said. We were in the garden. Here I said Let me show you and I got up and I touched her arm until she got up and then I held her hand and we moved, one step at a time, into the house.

She said I feel like there's something in me that shouldn't be there. We were in bed. I did not know what to say to that. What do you mean I said. She pressed herself into me and tried to bury herself in my arms. I turned her head towards mine. Are there feathers in your mouth? Why would there be feathers in my mouth. Have you I asked Been doing things with birds? Like what she said. I said like keeping them warm in your mouth. Or alternately eating them. Or dancing with them in the kitchen. I may have done that she said. When you were out.

I reached deep down her throat into her stomach and pulled out a gigantic bird. It moved on outside and waited for us. I took all of her teeth out of my arm and put them in my own mouth and kept them safe. She threw herself over my shoulder like a bath towel. I ran at the bird with the best of intentions.

—Why did you run at the bird
—I thought it would eat us and take us home

—What made you think this was not home
—It seemed like the thing to do

—What did this have to do with seeing the bird dancing with her earlier
—I don't know

—Seen through the window
—

—They were moving slowly. It sounded like Patsy Cline. The bird was holding her and she was holding the bird. You were just walking past on your way in.

—When I opened the door the bird disappeared. Her back was to me. What are you doing I said. Feathers spilled out of her mouth and spelled nothing. I saw something in the window and it seemed distant. I wanted to go there. I remember her telling me once how she would be borne away on the backs of birds.

—Then what happened

SASHA FLETCHER's novella ***when all our days are numbered marching bands will fill the streets and we will not hear them because we will be upstairs in the clouds*** (from which this story is excerpted) is due out from ***ml press*** in December of the year 2010. Sasha is an MFA candidate in poetry at Columbia University in the city of New York.

in the rooms where the women wait, there is little space for movement. chandeliers hang low from ceilings, iron-wrought and bristling with crystal, their shadows cast like crumpled spiders smeared across the walls. sharp-edged prisms swing like pendulums so that the women must stoop when walking, passing warily beneath the dripping wax and flames.

the rooms are named for functions: sewing, sleeping, bathing, dining, but most are reserved for sitting. footstools heavily upholstered. divans brocaded in arabesque. to differentiate these rooms from one another, the women try substituting synonyms for sitting. there is the crouching room, the squatting room, the perching room, the cowering room, the roost. there are also many rooms for waiting.

there is not a space left unfurnished, a wall unpapered, a side table unadorned. no sooner is an area cleared than it is filled again. a conspiracy of objects, refusing to give way. the women seek out furtive corners, nooks and niches, where they can breathe and clear their minds. they guard small sanctuaries of space, constructing false compartments, hidey-holes, trap doors. leave teacups overturned on the étagère, emptiness gestating within the bowled china bellies.

wherever they turn, the women are surrounded by gilt. it rims their saucers, glimmers from the wall clocks. sometimes they pick at the gold leafing, peel it back, take comfort in a surface stripped bare.

there is the resting room, the swooning room, the lounging room, the sprawl. replete with plush settees, nesting tables, hidden trundle beds. every object chosen to encourage opulent recline. the duvets and larders overstuffed, the hallways blocked by hampers.

the living rooms inhibit movement, encourage the inhabitants to dwell, to lodge, to bide. there is no rumpus room in which to roughhouse. there are no lofts, no towers or spires, nothing to encourage ascent. only a single story, with a root cellar below. the women climb the stunted stairway from the cellar to the living quarters in order to keep their muscles limber, to recall the feel of rising.

the rooms are crowded with armoires, highboys, chiffoniers, but not a single escritoire. the drawing room offers no tools for drawing. the study, nothing to study. the library is filled with decorative books, devoid of pages, hollow boxes holding only glue and dust. their covers sealed shut, much like the doors and windows.

the women fashion writing implements. they empty vases of pussy willows and peacock feathers, pull off silver buds and iridescent plumes in order to reveal sleek green branches, light and hollowed quills. sharpening tips into nibs.

the women steep teas, crush flower petals, mix the coagulated juice of fruits into ink. bereft of blank spaces, the women learn to write with baroque flourishes, in order to fit their words between the wallpaper's crowded arabesques. they stitch messages into crewelwork, tat words into lace. they needle holes into lampshades, writing texts in pointillist patterns of light.

in the changing room, the women practice transformation. tossing clothes onto lacquered butterfly tables, stripping down to skin. they smooth the pleats out of petticoats and write on the wide white surfaces. they yank the tongues out of shoes and pen poems along the narrow strips of leather. removing whale-bone stays from corsets if their quills splinter or snap. the bones deliver ink differently, inspire different forms of text. each writing surface calling forth specific syllables as the women rewrite, unwrite the rooms they sit in, the spaces they have begun to shape.

NINA SHOPE Nina is the author of *Hangings: Three Novellas*, published by Starcherone Books. Her writing has appeared in *Open City*, *3rd Bed*, *Fourteen Hills*, *Salt Hill* and on *sidebrow.net*.

Good.

Bury it, burn it, solder it together, wear it for a while and then leave it in its shape, submerge it in water, leave it on the dirt, in the sun, in the wind, in the rain, let the dew fall on it in the morning from the rooftop; if you don't like it as it is, wash it and it will turn into something else. Or you can felt it, sew it, embroider it, mold it, sculpt it, shape it, heal it, unweave it, knot it, weave it back together in another shape, paint it, set it on ice and let it melt into itself. Set it by a river, set it in the dirt, put animal bones in it, hair in it, leaves in it, keep it as a keepsake on your wall, ask other people to perform it, ask other people to hold it or caress it or treat it like a mother or a child, and don't interfere when they treat it like a lover, because it's in our nature to change the shape of things, to turn every bit of earth and material into memory, or salve.

When dolls have sex on the screen, and the hands hold the dolls, I feel uncomfortable. One is just a ghost-doll, and one is a real doll. The ghost doll has an open mouth. The ghost doll is starving for something. The real doll has brown hair, and climbs on the ghost doll, which is what happens in real life sometimes, the crawling yearning of it—which isn't always pretty. But sometimes, like at the end of the doll serenade, it is so good.

She was always cutting these pieces off of me, and this was at a time when I did not know that I could tell her: "Don't cut that piece off." So I let too much of myself go. First, before she cut, she burned. She'd focus on each little circle, raised bumps on my body, all over my body—behind my knees and at my hips and all along my stomach. Sometimes they ran in rows. Sometimes they were sporadic. Sometimes I saw pictures in their shapes, and the pictures would emerge the way constellations do when you look with someone who knows more than you do about the sky, and he points out each star, and then says, "See? A pogo stick," and you say, "Ahhhh." It was like that, except that it was my own body I was looking at, and I didn't like the dots. They were ugly and shameful, and I knew I was the only one who had them and I did not understand why I had to get them. I thought that I must be very bad to get to the dots. Finally, after months of being burned and cut, I was so tired, and I had all these dark circular scars across my skin, and my skin was sore, and always bleeding a little, covered in band-aids and tinged yellow from the disinfectant, and I was always worried about when the new dots would appear. I would check the mirror each morning to see: Had I gotten any more? Oh, crud, yes, three. I would call her and she would say, "Come on in and we'll burn and slice you," and I wouldn't tell any of my friends because I was so ashamed of my dots. I slid off to see her in secret, and had my dots cut in secret, and then covered the wounds with bandages and pants and long-sleeved shirts. And finally, I thought, There must be some other solution here. This is archaic. And it was archaic. It was nineteen-eighty-eight, for crying out loud. I was close to being bled. Leeches. Those old stories you hear. So I found a man who specialized in little dots across the body, especially the raised dots—he'd done a study of it, over the course of twenty years, and published the study in the extremely prestigious journal published by the Academy of Dots and Dermatological Malformations. I found it in the library, and it was a surprise because I did not know that there was a study about this, or a school that taught people about it, or even a library that held all these secrets that could unlock me, that could save me. I always thought the library was the same as the fire station. Brick. With sirens inside. And once I knew that there were other people out there with dots, I began to feel less ashamed, and less all-alone in my bandages and long-sleeved shirts even through the summertime. I called the man who published the study, and I said, "I think I have the dots you wrote about," and he said, "Tell me a little bit about yourself," and I said, "Well I am ten, and I go to Drew Elementary." He said, "All right, I'll see you." We made an appointment. And when I saw him, in my little white gown that was opened in the back, he looked at my dots, and touched them with his fingers—not even with gloves on like the other woman had, when she burned me and looked disgusted by my dots—and he said, "Yup, these are dots all right." And I said, "How will you take them off of me?" And he looked at me for a long time, and I saw that he was a very old and very kind man, because he did not look away, not once, even though he knew that I could be carrying this disease around with me through the world, could be passing it on to all the other people in the world. He said, "Look down." And I did, and

I saw: all my constellations had bloomed into flowers, dogwood white scattered on my body, around my bellybutton, up each leg, winding across my hips and up to my back. And I cried because it was beautiful and not those ugly dots I'd always known. And then, as I kept looking, the flowers started to fade, and disappear into the air, and I cried, and all that was a left was skin. So I was just myself, a regular ten year old again, maybe for the first time in my life. "How did you do that?" I said. And he said, "You were misinformed. It was buds, waiting to bloom." And I said, "So they didn't have to cut them off of me, all this time? And burn me? And try to kill little slices of me, shave them off bit by bit?" The old man shook his head and looked sad, and touched his forehead with one hand. "If only all the people knew," he said. "Are you scared now?" I said, "No, not anymore. I wouldn't even mind if they came back." He nodded. "That's the point," he said. "That's why they're gone." And then I was in my clothes, and on the street with the big elm trees overhead, and I was walking home, feeling strange and naked and light.

Once, I was a peanut-butter truck, and I smelled good inside. Everyone wanted to drive me because I reminded them of things they liked: moments when their mothers were nice, the sound of naptime, bananas, sticky tongues that made words all wrong. And laughing. They liked to laugh. When I was a peanut-butter truck, I think I made a lot of friends, but I could never tell if they were real friends, or if they just liked me for my peanut-butter. They got it free, and they could even, if they wanted, swim in it, because of the big vats that were taken wholesale to the cafeterias and the sick wards, where people needed peanut-butter to get better. Sometimes, they just waved as I drove by, and sometimes they turned away, because not-remembering something good can hurt less than remembering it.

Jettisoned against the sky, his ankles were weighted in water. So he was in between sky and water all the time, and he didn't like it, and he had breasts, which was strange to him, because he didn't think he should. But his friends said, "It's okay, man, some of us have breasts," and so he tried not to question whether or not he should. Anyway, he liked his friends, and he thought it was nice of them to feel him through this the way they did, this understanding they had of what he'd need when he realized that he had breasts and they did not. His friend Hank said, "Well some guys got man-boobs," and Villandros, our protagonist, said, "No. These are real and actual breasts. Like I have touched on other people." And Hank said, "You mean on women," and Villandros said, "Is that what they're called?" Sometimes people jeered at him, people who read his story and didn't believe that he might not know the difference between the sexes, that there were two, and that he was a man. Mostly. Sometimes people could be so cruel. But he kept at it, this imagining of himself as normal, as someone who was not a freak for being jettisoned, and not a freak for having parts that seemed like they ought to belong to someone else, or that were garish, somehow, on him. So he was grateful for their kindness, and not angry, and sometimes he looked into the water and saw how beautiful it was, and how beautiful his body looked beneath it, and he imagined that someday maybe he'd step outside the water, too, and see his body in the plain old air, and understand that it was good.

Big shapes on the wall in screaming faces, pink, and some boobies, he says, and some fingers up assholes, he says, which he thought was great when he saw it in nineteen-ninety-nine. He laughs. Everyone else laughs. People laugh when they see fingers jammed up assholes. Dreams of childhood are red and pink and green and blue, and cartoon-like, and layered, everything layered—the shapes and the stand-alones on the floor in front of the shapes, repeating themselves, maybe because memories repeat themselves, over and over in our lives, or maybe just because it is representing something that happened, which I do not know. This is art on the slide show, on the wall, this is art in the dark auditorium that was once a church. This is art in the green hills, in the dreamscape of a future I have wanted always, where nothing is hidden or too quiet, or fearful or ashamed, where everything is laughter and the sound of a river, and it fills me like water.

Rachel May's writing has been published in *Green Mountains Review, Indiana Review, Cream City Review, Meridian* and other journals. She's recently finished a story collection and is at work on a novel and a collection of essays.

Provenance

It lifted with colors from across the water and throttled a sound from against our fields. It mutilated our children. It emptied over from itself inside the manner of our speech. It was beautiful. It marked our hands and crippled our trees and became the place where the sun appeared brightest. It reassured us. It taught us to dance. When it rattled we tapped our feet. When it sang we sang along. It raped our daughters and dirtied our waters. It buried a figment of the sky inside the ground beneath the lake. It mangled our animals. It darkened our mornings. Its body was mostly wind and the wind of it concealed our voices. We offered it bread and peelings of fruit and lit small candles off the sills of our walls. The wind of its body became fire. It burned from inside the river and we followed the smoke it became. It felled birds from their sidewise formations. It forgave us. It lopped our skin from against our bodies and we could see it inside our blood. It offered us nothing. It tangled our breath from inside the air and we could smell what remained of our bodies. We followed it nights as best we could beneath the uptilted lights of the heavens. It settled finally inside a basin between the hills we had yet to name. It grew smaller and hardly moved. It made a sound from an opening in its body. The opening grew wider and the sound became soft. We could see from the rim of the basin what appeared to be a face. We could not cripple or save or destroy it. We listened. We watched. The sound of it lifted among us and we gave the hills a name.

David McLendon is an Edward F. Albee Foundation Fellow. He is the founder and editor of *Unsaid*. He divides his time between Ann Arbor and Brookyln.

The Parable of Our Giant

Once upon a time, all our nerves are intertwined and we react to pain and joy—gross stimulus—in coordinated, gross ways. So we think we are connected and almost one organism. Gradually our nerves disentangle and we sit in the middle of empty rooms. Small portholes—or perhaps round, desert mirrors—allow us fleeting glimpses of others in identical cells. Then we each notice a trapdoor beneath us and, crawling through it, find a giant controlled by the sum of all our thoughts. I can't bid the giant do my individual will, but feel some relief to discover another unity, one without control. We all hover at our hatches, between the world of the one giant body and our lonely but familiar cells, seemingly paralyzed.

Eugene Lim is the fiction editor for the online magazine *HarpandAltar.com* and the managing editor of Ellipsis Press. His fiction has appeared in *The Brooklyn Rail, sonaweb, No Colony, elimae* and elsewhere. His novel *Fog & Car* was published in 2008 by Ellipsis Press. A chapbook *And then She Wakes Up* was published by Mudluscious Press in 2009. He works as a librarian in a high school and lives in Queens, NY.

The Study

One night, a family was sitting at the dinner table together, when the father, without so much as a word to his wife and children, rose from his chair and retired to the study. When he had been gone for some time, and the family's food had grown nearly cold, the mother excused herself from the table and knocked on the study door.

'Remember your food and family,' she said. Receiving no reply, the mother returned to the table, and urged her children to eat.

Soon, the study door opened, and the father emerged, dressed in women's clothing. At the table, he ate his cold food quickly, avoiding the eyes of his loved ones.

'Dear,' said the wife, 'What is the meaning of this?'

'There's a woman in the study,' said the father. 'She dressed me this way.'

'Nonsense,' said the mother. 'You dressed yourself that way.'

'See for yourself,' said the father.

The mother then rose from her chair, and without so much as a word to her husband and children, retired to the study. When she had been gone for some time, and the family's food had grown ever colder, the son excused himself from the table and knocked on the study door.

'Remember your food and family,' he said. Receiving no reply, the son returned to the table.

When the study door opened, the mother emerged, dressed in little boy clothing. At the table, she ate her food quickly, avoiding the eyes of her loved ones.

'Mother,' said the son, 'What is the meaning of this?'

'There's a little boy in the study,' said the mother. 'He dressed me this way.'

'Nonsense,' said the son. 'You dressed yourself that way.'

'See for yourself,' said the mother.

The son rose from his chair, and without so much as a word to his sister and parents, retired to the study. When he had been gone a long time, and the family's food had grown frigid, the father and mother let their eyes settle on the daughter.

'Aren't you going to remind your brother of his food and family?' they said.

'No,' she said.

'And why not?' they said.

'Because then it will be my turn in the study.'

'Don't you want to be dressed by someone strange?' they said.

'Of course,' she said, 'but if I enter the study, who will come knocking after me?'

'Not I,' said the mother.

'Not I,' said the father.

Just then a strange child entered the room, and took the empty place at the table. The child wore no clothing at all, but carried a rosebud in his teeth.

'Don't look to me,' he said.

The Spot

A young man lay in bed one night, petting himself ever so softly so as not to disturb his roommate, who lay beneath him on the bottom bunk. Once he had made his spot, he sighed to himself, rolled over, and fell fast asleep.

All that night the young man dreamed troubled dreams. In one, he was condemned to death by a faceless judge.

In another, his spot had seeped all the way through, and dribbled down onto his roommate.

In yet another, the Devil lay beside him, petting him with hands all full of tacks.

The next morning the young man opened his eyes, rolled over, and felt around for his spot, only to find that it had dried during the night. When he heard his roommate stirring beneath him, he wished him good morning.

'Good morning,' said his roommate.

'Did you sleep well?' the young man asked.

'Last night I dreamed three troubled dreams.'

'Tell them to me.'

'In the first,' said the roommate, 'I dreamed that I condemned a faceless young man to death.'

'In the second,' said the roommate, 'I dreamed that my face was all spattered with goo.'

'And I dreamed the opposite!' said the young man. 'But what was the third?'

'In the third,' said the roommate, 'I dreamed that the Devil slept beside me.'

'Let me ask you something,' said the young man, keeping very still. 'Did you pet yourself before bed last night?'

'Oh no,' said his roommate. 'No, no, no, petting oneself is sinful.'

'So you've never petted yourself late at night, while I am sleeping above you?'

'No,' said his roommate. 'I always have someone do it for me.'

'Who then?' said the young man. 'Who's there to pet you?'

'Why, the Devil,' said his roommate.

'Oh,' said the young man, very softly. 'And does he have tacks all in his hands?'

'Oh yes,' whispered his roommate. 'Yes, yes, yes he does.'

THE BROTHERS GOAT reside below the bug line. They first met along a moist road, after this century had already turned. Still, there was something stunted about their encounter that evening.

two from A DICTIONARY OF HUES

Amber \ ˈam-bər\ *n* : the long-awaited melding of Will and Hunger. It is said in Huedom that so serene was the fusion that upon infecting one another for the first time Will and Hunger neither spoke, nor kissed, nor slipped into the mire of fictitious hopes.[1] Rather, becoming one another, they sifted through the earthen soil, penetrating the mantle, seeking the heat of the inner core, and retaining only themselves or perhaps something less (an unmistakable form of nudity). Once within, they concentrated and forgot what it means to Will and how it feels to Hunger. And, in forgetting, *that-which-once-could-Will* and *it-which-once-was-Hunger* invented sleep; they created twilight; and with the surplus mist from their muted breaths painted the whole of their invention a color only blearily remembered: Amber.[2]

This union did not proceed unregarded above the Earth's surface. Trees were the most sensitive to Amber's birth, their tellurian antennae sensing the Amber waves emanating from within the fecund orb. Several old magnolias were quick to oblige the editors of this hueology, informing us that everything—from their deepest roots to the highest blossoms—was thrown into a massive and pervasive *Amberuin*. As one arboreal witness said: "We might have been outside, that is, outside of where the color was being born, but really we were right there, we were inside *Kantrau Bau ambaru een sahn laigh*."

The account of another magnolia is more specific: "Oh, we knew something was astir down there in that place where the rocks flow like tree-sap in June. We knew the Earth was sprouting up something powerful. Hell, we had a month of dusk, a month of fixed Amber twilight."

Apparently, then, all was Amber: infinitely, smoothly, nudely Amber.

---

[1] Will and Hunger are both genetically incapable of such haze.
[2] This invisible birth of Amber has proven prototypical in that, since its emergence from the interior in 27 A.S. (After Sky), the birth of corporeal things (including aquarium fish, flying squirrels, domesticated birds, and huemans) has occurred just as it did in the case of Amber: an act of profound oblivion, a tribute to the power of unreason, and proof of the necessity for all things to swallow and be swallowed.

ii) Concerning the hue's civic history, Amber's cool embers are commonly accused of numerous transgressions, including passivity, excessive distance from the Three Glowing Winds,[3] and dilution of Brown.[4] Consequently, Amber has been severely persecuted during its ongoing and formative epoch. Eager to find fault with Amber, parishioners claim that its origin is fiction. A fairy tale. They claim that flowering trees everywhere are simply enamored and duped devotees of a guilty hue. The crux of their charge is that Amber engaged in parricide, not only in voiding the existence of its progenitors—Will and Hunger—but by flushing from itself every last trace of who Will and Hunger were prior to the inventions of sleep and twilight. Hueologists do not altogether dismiss such charges, questioning how else could the *stilljuice*, that lithic heme of Amber's petrified veins, remain so serene and so transparent. So devoid of Will. So devoid of Hunger.

iii) A school of hueological historians, the Benign Separatists, have proposed that the distance maintained between Amber and other prominent hues allowed Amber to weave one of the broadest sheets of visual serenity in all of Huedom.

iv) the only color that is customarily granted the privilege of political exemption from the affairs of the Chromatic Council, thus the only completely apolitical hue.

v) 14th century ME *ambregris*, from MF *ambre gris* gray amber, from ML *ambra*, from Ar *anbar* ambergris, a waxy substance found floating in or on the shores of tropical waters, believed to originate in the intestines of the sperm whale, and used in perfumery as a fixative.[5]

---

[3] The triumvirate consisting of Cobalt, Violet, and Virid.
[4] Hueologists have proven no genetic relation exists between Brown and Amber.
[5] Notice: All phonetic and etymological information in *A Dictionary of Hues*, except for that of "Nranchee" and "Sobak," is reproduced by permission from *Merriam-Webster's Collegiate® Dictionary, Eleventh Edition,* ©2003 by Merriam-Webster Inc. The date provided in the etymological portion of each entry refers only to the particular word's entry into the currency-language in use in this hueology—Immaterial Anglandish-and-Environspeak.

Beige \ˈbāzh\ *n* : the color of molars, of milk squeezed through a subterranean teat. All Beige fare is categorically claimed by that envious satellite, the Moon. Indeed, the white Moon swears all things Beige or just a bit on the dirty side belong, essentially, to it. Further, the Moon claims that anything that can turn White when infected with soap or time or sun or fear is just another piece of itself, stolen and stained by that highly self-conscious planet, Earth.

Not a simple problem, for though the Moon appears as tattered and expired as a prehistoric beggar, its albinic gaze bespeaks a living thirst and tormented need for the spill of a mammary. Indeed, it is only as tattered as it is hungry! For what are these valleys and craters but an accursed wealth of ulcerous stomachs and filleted tripe—empty, opened, and vacant.

As huemans, we must take a side (whether light side or dark side is up to you), and in doing so we observe that either the Moon is full of shit or—in its state of inanition—it has begun to confuse the call of colors. For, is the Moon truly white? Who among us has never turned skyward to the surprise of a Moon transformed, Beiger than Beige, seeming to kiss the eyes of Amber and violently caress the horizon's phosphorescent genitalia? Who has never once ventured out of their home, at dusk, only to be rapped by the visage of a globe dripping with sweaty yeses? What could one possibly do at such an ambushed moment but rail against the mind of Science, which assures us time and time again that "we need not fear that benign sphere wherein and whereupon only nothing grows."

Such are the words of sleeping beauties. Certified Hueologists, however, never fall for such assurances, for we, the scientists of colors, well know the disorder of hues: that which is Gray or White could never drip a drop of life such as the metachromatic Moon so often does into Beige and Orange and Copper and Ochre and Crimson and Rose or, most confoundingly of all, when its new cycle assumes the guise of Black; on the contrary, we know that which is Beige may, from far away, appear to have drowned in an achromatic breathlessness, thereby confusing and deceiving the color-blind into believing that we need not look with terror upon the sandswept parasite above. That never in a trillion years would it even dare to rot, or would it even think to stink.

We know the Moon is much more virtuous than this. We can see that the Moon is the master of perpetual decomposition, as cavernous and stenchful as the most putrid chunk of verminous cheese. *Beige* cheese.

ii) the color of waning honesty (see *Brown*).

iii) the color of everything scorned by transcendence, of all things that can only go from bad to worse, like teeth and divans in hotel lobbies.

Lito Elio Porto teaches literature and writing, most recently at UT. Austin and The New School. His publications include critical essays, political essays, poetry, and fiction, with recent work appearing in *Diagram* and *Action Yes*. His latest work is a book-length manuscript, *Outfitting Emptiness: Energy, Ecology, and Meaning*.

SLICING NAILS
(from THE NEW TECHNICAL MANUAL OF USE)

Because every pleasure and pain has, as one may say, a nail.
—PLATO

It may sometimes happen that in bent houses—houses that have transitioned into non-referential space—a Slicing Nail becomes lodged in a kitchen drawer. You pull on the drawer, and find that the grotesquely oversized nail acts like a jamb,[1] preventing the drawer from opening. What's more, the act of trying to open the jambed drawer causes the Slicing Nail to penetrate through the back of the drawer, and into the house-space, which is highly volatile. The house space may simply leak out—a slow, painful process accompanied by a menacingly high-pitched squeal; or the house space may burst into flames.

Proper removal, then, is essential.

Shore Edge and Moon Edge

Slicing Nails are composed of a Shore Edge and a Moon Edge. The Shore Edge is the outside, convex part of the nail. If the nail was severed from a healthy common nail, the Shore Edge will, as the name suggests, appear as a shoreline, changing from sandy-white to nearly translucent.[2] Often, the Shore Edge is coated with a thin, opaque layer of grit. After the Slicing Nail has been completely dislodged, the grit can be wiped away; however, exercise caution as the grit may contain trace amounts of harmful oils, fats, paints, particles, & etc, which can cause serious illness and infection.

The convex, Moon Edge, will be thicker, and flat, rather than sharp. This is where the Slicing Nail was severed from the common nail. It will usually be either serrated or smooth. Serration occurs when the nail

[1] In fact, Slicing Nails are more fragile than they might appear. While a forceful tug may open the drawer, the Slicing Nail will surely be broken.

[2] If the Common Nail was unhealthy, the nail may appear yellowish or even brown or black. It will have a flakey, brittle appearance, and will not be suitable at all for later use. The outlined steps may still be used for extraction—however, it is recommended that after extraction is complete, one should dispose of the sickened Slicing Nail.

was separated by biting, tearing, or the much more infrequent Tiberius condition:

Before he got out of the house, he stumbled against the threshold. The blow was so severe that the nail of his great toe was broken and the blood ran out through his shoe.
—PLUTARCH

A smooth edge indicates that the nail was cut from the common nail with the aid of scissors or clippers.

Sometimes there will be a milky-white residue where the Moon Edge was severed. If the Slicing Nail has been lodged for some time, the residue may have dried, and will appear as a dusty white powder. In some traditions, the substance, also called Moon Dew, is collected for its salve-like properties. Steam distillation of Moon Dew produces an essential oil that can be used as a fragrance in perfumes, soaps and food, and for aromatherapy.

Sought whiter draughts, with dipping finger-tips
They pressed the sod, and gushing from the ground
Came springs of milk.
—EURIPIDES

It can also be boiled into a tonic, or added to soups and stews as a thickening agent.

Extraction

Once the Shore Edge and Moon Edge have been established, one may extract the Slicing Nail. Even a healthy nail can be broken. Be gentle, and you will be rewarded with a Slicing Nail that will last a lifetime.

Simply yanking the Slicing Nail from where it has punctured the inner House Space will result in House Space deflation or combustion, as mentioned above.

Nail-plough'd the furrows bleed
The while on cries of pain
—AESCHYLUS

In order to avoid this catastrophe, plaster the area around the nail with a thick mash of magazine gluten.[3] The type of magazine gluten used is not important, though coloring-book gluten tends to be too thin, while fashion gluten is almost unworkable. Stick with the more all-purpose glutens: tabloid, food & beverage, outdoor, or even craft. These tend to have a more balanced ratio of picture to text.

Fortify the gluten with a tablespoon or two of methylcellulose. This will stretych your drying time so that, when the Slicing Nail is removed, the still-wet magazine gluten will seep into the evacuated space. When the gluten mash hardens, the House Space will be precautionarily sealed. (Though magazine gluten is typically archival, it is useful to check the patch for cracks or leaks after a week or so.[4])

Now, grip the Slicing Nail gently. Even though there is a good chance that the Slicing Nail had been worked and dulled prior to being clipped or broken from the common nail, it's possible that the Shore Edge is still razor sharp. Either test the edge, or play it safe and wear heavy-duty gloves.

Begin wiggling until you feel the nail give. If the Slicing Nail continues to resist your efforts, the nail may be intractable—this happens when a serrated (bitten) edge catches on the lip of the house space, preventing extraction. If this is the case, the only foolproof method for extraction is the Tick Method[5]—unfortunately, this may render the Slicing Nail all but useless.[6]

Care

After the Slicing Nail has been extracted, there are a few final steps to take before it can be put to use in the kitchen. First, the top or bottom (for the most part, interchangeable) of the Slicing Nail must be wrapped in heavy, leather strop. This will be used as a handle, preventing the hand from being cut.

---

[3] Magazine Gluten is relatively easy to make (assuming you do not already have it on hand). Any magazine will work, but glossy magazines, full of colorful pictures, seem to work best. Simply shred the magazine, and boil it in a sufficient quantity of water, until a thick, manageable paste forms.

[4] An easy way to check is to place a dollop of soapy water over the hole. If bubbles form, you can be sure of a leak, and repatching will be necessary.

[5] Acid is used to dissolve the impacted area of the Slicing Nail, allowing it to be freed.

[6] Expert nail-smiths are sometimes able to reshape broken Slicing Nails into Lesser Nails. Some argue, however, that the tensile strength is irrevocably compromised.

Next, one must determine the style in which the Slicing Nail was set. If the nail is in the American style, the Shore Edge will have a soft, microscopic tooth to it, which will make for relatively easy re-sharpening on a traditional steel. In fact, the dullness of an American Slicing Nail actually refers to the bending of the microscopic barbs. Steeling serves to stand the barbs up again. Japanese-style Slicing Nails, on the other hand, have a relatively hard tooth. These cannot be steeled—the microscopic teeth would be broken, leaving the nail dull and useless. Japanese-style nails must be carefully re-sharpened (honed) on a proper wet-stone.

The only foolproof method of discovering the style of the Slicing Nail is to look at it under a microscope. However, there is a method, which, nine times out of ten, yields positive results.

> *Whatever things are joined together by glue, or by a nail, or by a chain, are one thing, but contains in itself the cause of its own continuity.*
>
> —ARISTOTLE

By holding the Slicing Nail up to the light, one should see either that the nail is nearly translucent, or one may detect a slightly wavy pattern, almost like the ripples of a sand dune. The ripples indicate that the nail has been damasticated, meaning that it was formed from a very large sheet, which was then folded in on itself many many times. Damastication provides for the extremely hard teeth of the nail, and is used primarily in the Japanese style. Thus, if the wave pattern is detected, it is very likely that your Slicing Nail is Japanese.

Finally, some authorities recommend the application and reapplication of soapstone to prevent calcification. This can be done when it seems that the moon edge is becoming too dry. Once the Slicing Nail has been properly wrapped and treated it is ready for use.

ADAM WEINSTEIN lives and writes and grows vegetables in Tuscaloosa, Alabama, with his wife Emily, and their cat, Swordfish. *The New Technical Manual of Use*, a collection of essays on which he is hard at work, is his wunderkabinett.

Carnegie Nail

Doubtless, early on, in the ultra-fine beginning of the day, others were spectators as I withdrew into Carnegie Nail and I showed the coarseness of my nature in a new sense, for I kept my hands forever forward until at Mrs. Oh's behest, Dee took them.

As a courtesy, to some extent, Mrs. Oh kept her cell phone conversation brief and her voice low.

Mr. Oh sat unspeaking in an aimless, I mean, armless chair. He was less muscular than I would have expected—composed, nonetheless, of curving segments. Then, as if by the flip of a lever, he fell from his chair.

Others jumped around.

Strangest of all, whoever enters Carnegie Nail is exempted from the bitterness of experience.

Oh, Mr. Oh found his way back up to good effect while Mimi supported the shop's potted, toppled plant.

Dee resembles me—especially her faint eyebrows and her thick, pomaded, smoothed-back hair. She dug deftly into my fingertips in the time we had remaining.

The damp day got me as I left, but I did not publicly condemn it.

At home Wanda appeared with our infant and the infant's father—my husband—was seated in a chair that's sufficient to defend itself.

My next step surely was clear, for life presents the flowers of life. We'd been viewing the infant as if it'd been wrenched off a tree branch or a weedy stem.

But the question is much more complex. A child needs to be cut down to its lowest point compatible with survival.

Diane Williams's most recent book is ***It Was Like My Trying to Have a Tender-Hearted Nature.*** She was awarded a 2010 Pushcart Prize. She is the founder and editor of the literary annual *NOON*.

THE LONESOME DEATHS OF BUD AND SANDY

1.

Dad: 'I'm going to drown Bud now, son. You distract my friend Walt.'
Sandy: "Okay, Dad.'

Dad: 'I'm going to throw you in the water and drown you.'
Bud: 'Okay, Dad.'

Dad: 'Why won't you die?'
Bud: 'I'm trying, Dad.'

Sandy: 'Hit him on the head with the anchor, Dad.'
Bud: 'Try hitting me between the eyes.'

Dad's friend Walt: 'I can't believe Bud's dead.'
Sandy: 'I thought his face would be frozen in a silent scream. But it's still cool.'

2.

Sandy: 'Being eaten alive by a shark is not cool. I don't care what anybody says.'
Dad: 'But it looks fantastic, son. I guess that's what I meant by cool.'

Dad's friend Walt: 'I wish there wasn't so much blood. It's hard to see anything.'
Bud: 'Sandy, are you still alive? 'Cos I have a suggestion. Oh, no, I guess you're not.'

Bud: 'Shoot the shark in the head or something, Dad. It's getting away.
Dad: 'Will do, son.'

Dad's friend Walt: 'Why do you want to keep the shark, Bud?'
Bud: "Cos I want to cut it open and see what Sandy looks like now.'

DENNIS COOPER is the author of eight novels. His most recent book is a collection of short fiction, *Ugly Man* (Harper Perennial). Hés the editor of the Little House on the Bowery imprint for Akashic Press. He currently lives in Paris where he maintains a blog, co-creates theater works with the French director Gisele Vienne and the musician/composer Stephen O'Malley (Sunn0))), and is working on a new novel about a twenty-two year old French cannibal.

The Men From Life

I have a photograph, and in it, my much older friend and I sit at the foot of a hotel bed. Also in the photo are men from LIFE magazine. They ask my older friend, not me, questions.

"How did you two meet?" one of the men from LIFE asks. My older friend says, when he had first met me, I had smelled proudly of the carnival and still had smoking lapels.

My older friend answers all the questions the men from LIFE have.

He's responsive, honest, my older friend. Says he masturbates into his socks and is sorry for the launderer. Says he taped a pinwheel to his mailbox and has me look for letters only when it spins.

"What kinds of letters do you get?" the men from LIFE ask.

"Acceptances," my older friend says.

He says I won't take him home at times because I'm afraid he will break his antique furniture. He says he's been on three models of ambulance and never calms when in jail.

As an undergraduate, he had kept slim by clutching train tracks and dancing

The men from LIFE take notes and sketches. They take pictures. They call for whiskey, ice, services.

"You drink, do you?" the men from LIFE ask him.

"I eat ice," he says.

He says he was once a pin lifter—that he would pick diamond sticks off necks, heads, and chests.

He'd had a wealthy suicide father, but the man had left him nothing but a small name, something whispered, something that meant no ancestry.

He says his mother had had him lift the bottoms of her breasts and that he never liked that electric lights disturb shade trees.

"Call us 'pal,'" the men from LIFE say. "Say 'Ah.' Say 'O.'"

In the photo that I have, at the foot of the bed, my older friend and I cross our legs over our thighs. It looks as if we're seeing who has the slimmest hips.

This older friend of mine is a sleek man, tweedy, a talker. He wears elegant overcoats and worsted suits. He favors fountain pens. He likes to steer.

"Two to six inches of ash covered everything," he says, responding to the questions of the men from LIFE.

He shakes his head, continues.

He explains how the sailors of the day knew nothing of a certain volcanic eruption. For them, between spars and ropes and their arms, the sky too quickly became gray, the sea gray. Strange fine grains collected at the backs of their throats. They felt as if they no longer sailed on the sea but, instead, trundled on the soggy ground. On an island beneath a shuddering mount, thousands of upset purple centipedes scuttled into a sugarcane refinery. Snakes, out from porous rocks and into muddy streets, went for tailored hems, tanned shins. Horses suffocated on sulfur air. Black rain. Black clouds with 1,000° of Farenheited steam. Only a few people survived—one was a man locked in an underground prison for a tawdry bar fight. He joined Barnum & Bailey after, became famous for living. He never had to touch a trapeze's bar or a big cat's tooth. He just had to stand while the audience imagined 50,000 dead. "The Man Who Survived Doomsday!" lived to see Troy, Baltimore, Detroit, beans on his plate, clam bouillon.

The men from LIFE pose my older friend. They have him put his foot up on the windowsill, the radiator, the bathtub. They have him sit on the end of the bed with me.

"Why don't you pretend to write something!" the men from LIFE say.

"I could write something," he says.

"Why don't you *pretend* to write something."

He says he once saw an entire discarded Victorian staircase at a dump in New Jersey. He pretends to write something. *Famous for living.*

The men from LIFE leave.

I sleep in the hotel bed. My older friend rides a taxi, waves to a stranger, and jumps off a bridge. But he doesn't drown in a river that's gone scummed at the edges. He doesn't die of trauma. He suffocates on the air—as if there is something material in it. Later, people find his name etched carefully into his necklace. In one of his shoes, they pick out his name on a check I had made out for him. It's for rent. And the men from LIFE, they soak their silvered images.

ELLIOTT STEVENS grew up in Hawaii and spent his summers in New Jersey. A story of his has appeared in *elimae*, and another is forthcoming in *NOON*.

Bathhouse in 5 Senses

Colors:
Inside, it's never morning. Red doors and black hallways lit by pale yellow like a house by candles, minus the flickering. In ulterior stairwells, the bright mobile overhead casts a lattice, dances, the black cut through with woven, streaking white. The hot tub, a polyhedrous expanse with tight, shadowed corners of pale, quivering blue. The skin of the men—all three of them—is brown, in graded shades. The last's furred with soft black hairs, front and back, and when I clutch his shoulder, I discover the latter is far less revolting than I had generally assumed.

Sounds:
Stalking these hallways, one expects to hear ecstasies. Perhaps men swallow their moans like Mormon teenagers jacking off within earshot of their parents. Perhaps their moans are drowned by the drone of drained techno. I hear the third man say, "Maybe we should take a break." I say, "Yes, let's take a break," and lay my head down on the pillow. He says, "This is my room." "Oh," I say. "Right." And stagger across the hall.

Smells:
I do not smell the first man's semen because he came inside his condom. I do not smell the second's because it puddled on my lower back, and I am not that flexible… yet. When the third man doesn't finish, I smash my nose into bleached sheets.

Tastes:
Peppermint pipes through the water fountain. The men taste like candies tongued after dinner, sucked from twisted cellophane. Pubic hairs through my teeth are flavorless floss. Later, in the bathroom, I'm belching rancid beer. Fading, I glug a Monster, but it isn't delicious, 11 quarters I'll never get back.

Textures:
My towel chafes my haunches and genitals too. Whenever I remember to notice, I'm strafed by something tiny and rough. Latex, seeming smoothish, when jackhammered isn't. "Ow!" I say, but not out loud. The hair on the first man's scalp is wooly, but when I touch his belly to apologize for cuddling, it jiggles underneath my hand.

Tim Jones-Yelvington lives and writes in Chicago. His work has appeared or is forthcoming in *Annalemma, Pank, Keyhole, Monkeybicycle* and others.

And Given the Chance to Be Safe

The son looked into the bowl. In the bowl was clear, clear water.

When looking into the bowl the son usually saw just, already and always water.

Never would he look in the eye of what came out of him and stuck itself in the bowl, against it.

The son had clogged the toilet. Somehow, and he was not sure how.

Stuffed it full, but of what he couldn't name.

The bowl remained clear and empty of all but water.

He tried to flush it and the handle wouldn't descend to flush, even in his grip, his soft and terrified hand.

This clog from elsewhere, otherwise said, this clog without a source.

No source that the son would call "his."

The water certainly, no, was not his water, water from him.

He trundled downstairs and woke up the parents in their sleigh bed.

"This is a nice sleigh bed, I sleep well in it," the father would say before saying, "good night."

After "good night" the son would often, recently, have dreams of the father asleep in his sleigh bed, just asleep, unmoving and without a sound.

After "good night" it was true that the father lied, he was a liar and he did not go to sleep, because how could he sleep when he was so loud and red to the mother, and well it was true that the mother was loud and red in exchange, and things happened like then the toilet choking itself.

The father probably wore shoes to bed.

The son woke up the parents in their sleigh bed.

He knew it was not good but this was an emergency for everyone.

Not just the son.

He stood in the doorway and made his face like a Q.

He made small sounds, as small as he could make them.

So it would look like he was just standing around and making small sounds in the dark.

Like a ghost but he was so used to making small sounds to rouse the parents that he felt he could not disappear, unlike a ghost.

But after all ghosts cannot disappear or they would not be ghosts, the grandmother would tell him.

The son did not agree.

The father fought his way up and, shirtless, crushed full of hair, he said to the ghost in the doorsill, "Hey what the fuck is this about."

"Nothing."

The mother hit her fists around in the dark and said, "What, what, what."

The son said, "It isn't a big deal."

"Come on, I have to go to work early, I am asleep," the father said, tightening red already.

"Please it isn't a big deal."

"What, come on, I'm asleep now, it's so late, I'm going to be so tired in the morning," the mother said.

"Shut up now," the father said to the mother.

"Please I just stuffed the toilet, please."

"Fuck, I don't believe this," the father said.

"Make him unclog it," the mother said.

"I will show him how to unclog it. I will show him how to be a man."

"I want to be a man."

The caravan of father, mother and son grabbed a plunger and went upstairs into the son's bathroom.

The father swung the plunger around and acted like he was fighting people at work.

"This is what happens when I go to work on Sundays."

"Hey, look, I am fighting you," he said to the mother.

The mother patted the son and said something neither of them knew what.

"I'm going to unplug the toilet, I'm going to go to sleep, and I'm going to charge you all money like I'm a plumber," the father said.

The father soaked his hands.

He fondled the plunger.

The mother looked like how she did when she talked on the phone to her ex-husband.

Her ex-husband was in charge of the son's half-brother, the other son.

She was red like the father, but not all the way red.

She was red like when the father found pictures of her that he waved around the house.

Her ex-husband, called "Subzero" by most people.

Subzero was in most of the pictures.

The son had seen them and stolen some of them

The father fixed the plunger to the bowl and moaned a little.

The mother snapped her hands to the father.

“Let me do it,” she said.

Both the mother and father did the plunging in shifts.

Their techniques were the same, firm and like sleepwalking.

The son watched and turned the same red as his father.

Ghosts are not red so I guess this is becoming a man.

“Let me do it again,” they kept saying.

Nothing happened to the water or the toilet any of the times.

The water stayed where it was mostly.

It splashed around a little.

After eight tries, four for each parent, the grandmother ed into the bathroom and smiled, this smile the transmission of what can only be called “the ‘and’ of ‘being and nonbeing.’”

“Mom, what are you doing awake?” the mother asked.

“Let me give it a go.”

“Mom, if we can’t do it you can’t, please,” the mother said.

“Just let me.”

The grandmother was old and soggy.

The son didn’t want her to see what he had done to the toilet was his immediate reaction.

“Don’t, grandma,” the son said.

“Let me,” the grandmother said.

The grandmother gathered the plunger from the father.

She snuck it perfectly into the toilet bowl and began to press and pull on it.

Her skin violently white.

A white like porcelain, incidentally.

The son began to cry and to say, "Grandma, no, you might get hurt."

"Grandma will not," the grandmother said.

The grandmother released the plunger and the water made a sound like swallowing itself and everyone thanked the grandmother and they went to bed in disbelief and the toilet wasn't clogged again for probably three years.

When the water had swallowed itself the grandmother had said, "Yee haw!"

Two months after unclogging the toilet the grandmother died of a disease in her heart.

After the grandmother died the real problems started.

Like, for instance, the mother often turning herself yellow instead of red, and the mother ringing the doorbell and yelling to the son who came to the door, let me in this is my house you are my fucking son aren't you and then driving the car through the facade of the house, and the father saying, "I didn't call for a car until five p.m.," and he laughed and then called all the police he could find.

Like, also, the son clogging the toilet intentionally like stuffing it with some ghost and then trundling down to the father's sleigh bed, now only the father's, and gathering the father and pulling him upstairs to look, look at this, look at this I clogged the toilet again, but the father will shake his head no, the grandmother is not coming, her face, you will realize one day when the whole thing overflows, is not remembered in the shades of your shit and piss, and the father will not plunge the toilet, he will not plunge the toilet anymore.

ALEC NIEDENTHAL can be found in *Agriculture Reader, Caketrain, Smokelong Quarterly* and elsewhere. He currently lives in Sarasota, Florida, where mostly it is hot and old.

The Vanished

The man had always aspired to live his life as inoffensively as possible, and when his woman came home one evening and found he was gone, she was sure for days that he was around there somewhere. Perhaps he had gone to the bathroom and was in there, quietly creaking, making silent curses over the pipes. Maybe he was in the attic. Or maybe he was working late, something he did not treasure but did with a kind of silent pride that suited him and had always bothered her.

After a few days, it became apparent that the man was not in the backyard or behind the television. She grew nervous, imagining how disappointed he might be upon returning to find that she had not kept the house clean. Indeed, she had forgotten she was in a house at all, and had scattered newspaper across the bedrooms and allowed branches to crowd the door. A thin skin of dust covered the bookshelves and countertops and toaster oven and toilet tank, her desk and his desk. It piled up like snowdrifts in the framed pictures on the wall. She tossed and turned in the bed until the covers parted and formed a protective whorl around her body.

The woman stopped leaving the house. She decided that if her man peeked through the window or knocked lightly on the door and realized that she had gone, he would leave for good. She ate all the fresh food in the house, and then all the canned food, and then the expired food, and then the spices. She washed tablespoons of cinnamon down with tap water. She reached out the windows, pulled leaves from the trees and ate them with the last of the salad dressing. She released the cats so that she would not eat them, and then she ate their food.

The man's father called to ask if there had been any updates, and to inform her that he had called the police. At the time of his call, the woman had been using a dainty flathead screwdriver to open the man's computer. She had wanted to see if the man had left any clues in there, but there was only more dust. She swallowed the computer's tiny screws.

It became apparent that the man had not taken any of his clothes with him. The woman knew that her man owned 3 black undershirts and 5 white, 7 pairs of jeans and 27 button-down shirts, 5 collared polo shirts,

4 t-shirts with silkscreened graphics and one novelty shirt that he only wore as a joke, a button-down two sizes too large and covered in neon images of ice cream and hot dogs. She could not bear to eat it but took it out of the closet and observed it every morning, salivating.

She ate all the pages out of his books.

When the detectives arrived, she apologized for her appearance. She explained that she was too worried to leave the house. She showed them the man's clothes and his personal effects. She took them on a tour of their home and showed them the toilet he used and the ironing board and the grill. The things were untouched, she noted, she had left them untouched. When the man came home, he would appreciate his things being untouched. He was very particular and appreciated her respect and in exchange, he showed her respect. The detectives looked at her distended belly and asked if she was pregnant. She cradled the mass and said that she was.

Things started arriving in the mail. There were bills and notices that the woman no longer understood. It seemed like someone was asking the man to pay a huge sum of money to a credit card and a house. She took all the paper money she had not yet boiled and stuffed it into the envelopes provided and sent them back.

Other letters were more troubling. There was a handwritten letter from the man's grandmother that didn't make any sense until the woman cut out all the words and rearranged it:

> TAKE WITH YOU ALL TIME TO WEATHER EXCELLENT PARTS. HELLO WORK TOGETHER UNTIL YOU UNDERSTAND WHAT YOUR FATHER TELL. LOVE YOUR WIFE THEN RETIREMENT. WARM DAYS FORGET NIGHTS. DON'T NEGLECT ENJOY MONDAY.

The woman thought that was all pretty good advice, and taped it to the refrigerator. She opened the refrigerator and ate the baking soda from its box with a spoon.

Some days later, the man's phone rang. He had left it plugged in when he vanished but his woman had not heard it ring before. When she heard it, she vomited into a small trash bin next to the phone. She could barely summon the strength to pull herself up to look at the phone. She couldn't make out the number displayed through the layer of dust. The phone's ring sounded like the old rotary phone her parents kept in their home. She wondered if it was the man calling his own phone, and why that would be. Perhaps she had gotten phones switched and was confused. The phone stopped ringing. The woman placed the phone in her lap, pried the number 2 from the keypad with a screwdriver, and ate it.

It was a terrible idea to go outside again. The woman had seen a couple out the front window and was sure that the man had placed them there for her to see. She banged her fists on the windows to try to get their attention but when they didn't make a move to acknowledge her, she threw open the locks on the door and rushed out.

The couple was a boy and girl couple, and they were eating love right out in the open. They swallowed great handfuls of love, sticky tangled masses of it, standing nose to nose with one another. They were gorging on the stuff. Love dripped from their hands and landed in spatters on their shoes. The boy wiped his hand in his hair and left a long slick. These gluttons of love spread it across each other's mouths. They made wet noises as they consumed.

The woman rushed up to the people and slapped the love out of their hands and said Don't eat that! That's poison! and the boy laughed but the girl looked at her unkindly and bent down to gather the ruined pile of love up from the ground. The woman watched the remainder seep across the asphalt.

Get a hold of yourself, the girl said. The girl clasped the slop to her chest. It bled through her shirt to her skin. Look at what you did, the girl said. The woman looked. She felt relieved, but of course it was not enough.

Amelia Gray is the author of *AM/PM*, published by Featherproof Books, and ***Museum of the Weird***, due Fall 2010 through Fiction Collective 2. She blogs at ameliagray.com.

Isaac, Isaiah, Ishmael

Even at birth they were already damaged, their brittle bones contraction-crushed, powdered by the mother's powerful organs, her pressing canal: All those tiny ribs snapped and splintered upon the stainless of the operating room steel. All those skulls crooked and cracked, all those twisted greenstick limbs. We lifted each child out from her body and into surgeries of its own, did our best to splint and screw our prides back together. So few survived, and for what next chance? On what legs would they stand, with no milk to grow them strong except from the body which had already failed to make them so?

If only there was some other mother, some second receptacle for the babies we want so badly to make. But no. There is only me and my brothers, only this one woman between us, captured alone long after we thought the pilgrims and refugees would come this way no more.

To quell my brothers' anger, to beg their patience, I say, This woman may not be capable of producing what heir we need, but perhaps she may yet birth the one who might, if only one of her daughters lives to have a set of hipbones strong enough to bear our advances.

And so we fill the mother with powdered milk, with canned peaches, with vitamin-paste squeezed from nearly empty tubes.

And so we fill her with meat.

Every new wish is followed by another wait, followed by another failure: Push, we say, our voices speaking in unison, our wants aligned after a lifetime of bitterest division, of brotherly strife. Together, we make what we can make, and we save what we can save. Push, we say, and then comes this next baby born just as broken, its first cry already choked with the chalk of its bones. Its newborn everything else shattering into dust. This daughter-like reminder that not all birthed into this world shall see it reborn, and then again our determination, our willingness to try once more.

And then, Lie still, I say, and then, Hold her, brothers, hold her, and then, I will plant again in her this seed, until at last we grow the fruits we desire.

Abelard, Abraham, Absalom

This smoldered cigar, last of a box of twenty. Bought to celebrate happier times. Smoked to keep away the smell. Of our unwashed skin, of our slipping flesh. Our baby grows in my wife's belly, submerged sign of a prophecy burning atop her hot hard bulge: All hair, just like the others. Gone wrong again, gone wrong again. Black hail spatters the house. Tiny fists, falling from the cloudless sky. Banging on the skin of our walls. Breaking windows to give access to broken beds. Our house fills with air the texture of mud, with black birds forgetting how to fly. Vultures and crows, waiting for our child. To make their nest of him. Mine eyes on shattered glass, on my wife's pelvis tilting toward sunlight. Sun the color of baby's first shit. Then the color of blood. Then the blood, flowing between her legs. Cigar smoked, held between loose teeth. Push. Push right now. A boy, just like the others. Hair on cheeks, on forehead, on lips and tongue. Inverse of our own nakedness. Shame in an equal and opposite amount. For baby, a name waiting out of a book of names, exhausted one after the other. Sequenced failure. Hook a finger into baby's tiny mouth and pull out hair, hairball. From furred windpipe. From matted esophagus. Only my wife cries. Only the birds caw, flap their wings. Only a howl of spoor, cigar sputter. Pull, my wife says. Pull. As if I could ever pull enough. As if I could ever clear the lungs of this fur. As if I could clear the stomach. As if I could clear the heart, its chambers full, clenched, wrong for what choked world awaits. Pull, she says. Pull. Pull. Pull. And what coward I would be to stop.

Matt Bell is the author of *How They Were Found*, forthcoming in Fall 2010 from Keyhole Press. His work in this issue is excerpted from an unpublished novella-in-shorts. He can be found online at mdbell.com.

GOOD NEWS

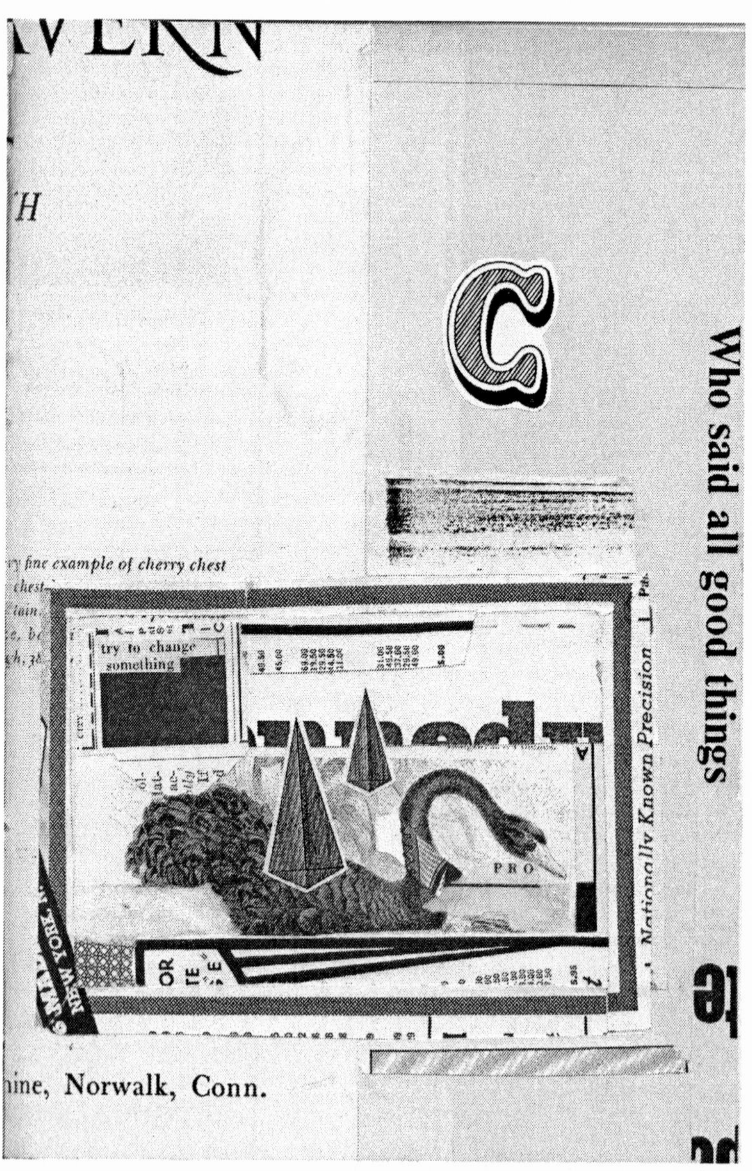

EDUARDO RECIFE is an artist/illustrator and designer from Brazil. You can check some of his works on the ever evolving website: www.misprintedtype.com / www.eduardorecife.com.

Called to Mr. Ganzfeld's office about midmorning on Tuesday, Jerry found him sitting at an oval desk wearing his balsa nose and trimming the hair on a doll's head. "Smell this, Chung. Smell the hair." He handed Jerry the doll's head. "We've been getting complaints."

"It does have an odor. Like laundry starch."

"Someone has been fucking my sheep. As every shepherd down the ages has learned, if you fuck them too much, the hair gets a stink. Who is it who's fucking my sheep? It's that new man, Billy Pong. You know him?"

"Ping. I see him around. We talk a little."

"Find out if he's the one. There's a bonus in it."

"I'll keep an eye on him."

"You find out who's been bestial with my wooly girls and I'll take you hunting at my country place. That's a promise."

"I'd really enjoy that, sir."

On leaving the office, Jerry noticed a black lambskin satchel sitting between two rosewood bookcases. It looked like a physician's medical bag. He'd been to the office several times before, but had never seen the bag. It was such an odd thing, he almost asked Mr. Ganzfeld about it, but changed his mind.

When he returned to the shearing line, Jerry saw Billy passing by, pushing a wheelbarrow piled high with sheep dung.

"Billy," Jerry whispered. "Stop a minute."

"How goes it, Mozit?"

"Fine, fine. Look, Ganzfeld thinks you've been dicking his wooly girls. Have you?"

"Who hasn't? If he thinks I'm the only one he's batty. Yeah, I tried it. I got kicked in the shins and she shat all down my boots. That was the last time."

"What am I supposed to tell Ganzfeld if he asks about you again?"

"Blame it on Digby. Big guy, red hair. Hasn't been to work in three weeks."

"I'll do that," Jerry said.

Mimi arrived back at the cottage an hour before Jerry got home from the Mill. She used the time to take a sitz bath with the last little bit of Epsom salts in the box. The little tub wasn't long enough for her to stretch her legs all the way, but sitting in the warm water with its salty feel on her skin was immediately relaxing. She lathered her close-cropped hair with fatted soap she'd taken from Ganzfeld's. The tub was close enough to the pellet stove that a kettle of water sat warming an arm's reach away for rinsing. Through the small window of the bathing area, she saw Jerry coming up the lane, still favoring his sore foot.

Before coming in, he shouldered a sack of pellets from the storage shed.

"Just in time," Mimi said. "The stove is almost empty."

"I'm so glad you're back. It's been months. How's your cousin?"

"He lingered on and on, but now he's dead."

"Your hair is shorter. Shouldn't it be longer by now?"

"Cousin Charlie's nurse is very handy with scissors. She cut it for me."

"I see you have some new soap."

"Also from Charlie's."

"Did he leave us anything?"

"The sheep, the land, the house, everything he left to Ganzfeld, in payment of some sort of debt."

"It all goes to him eventually, why not now?"

"Have you gotten along well enough without me, Mr. Chung?"

"Same ole, same ole. The wart's a lot better. I put out plenty bug powder. The new neighbor broke in. Ganzfeld's brother. Says he is anyway. He's got brain damage. Ganzfeld hit him with a shovel for organizing a union."

"I hope you're not thinking along those lines, Mr. Chung."

"Nobody's organizing anything. He thinks we are. So we're blaming it on Digby, some guy hasn't been to work in a few weeks."

"Well, Mr. Chung, I know where this Digby is. I was going to tell you. I saw a body in a shelter on the way back. There was a hole in his head and a gun in his hand. His tag said Digby. You should report that right away."

"A red-haired guy?"

"Very red."

Mimi toweled off. "I brought home some puffballs for dinner." She put on fresh clothes while Jerry loaded the stove with pellets. He was thinking he might go ahead and tell Ganzfeld that Digby was the one fucking his girls. If it was Digby out there in the shelter, and it wasn't reported, he would be found soon enough anyway. Meanwhile, things could be blamed on him.

On Wednesday afternoon Mr. Ganzfeld called Jerry to his office.

"Well, who is it? Is it more than one man?"

"One man, sir. That's what everyone says. Name of Digby."

"Digby then. I'll give him a talking to he won't forget."

"Yes, sir. Anything else?"

Ganzfeld stood. "Yes. Fucking my sheep is one thing. Fucking me and my Mill, that's another thing. I have good reason to believe someone is making moves toward organizing a worker's union. Keep an eye on things, will you? Look for someone with a dull nature. It's the perfect façade. Behind it you'll find the steely underpinnings of a dedicated communard."

"I'll see what I can find out."

On the walk home, Jerry spotted Billy having a Postum at Chow Fun's and writing in a notebook with a pencil stub.

"Billy."

"Jerry. How goes it Mozit?"

"Good enough. What's up, anything?"

"Nah. You?"

"Ganzfeld thinks somebody's trying to organize a union. I told you what he did to his own brother."

"You know it's not me."

"Me either."

"Blame it on Digby."

There were dead gnats floating on the surface of Jerry's Postum. He scooped them out with a spoon. "Any idea what happened to him? What's the word around the Mill?"

"They say he got despondent when his mother died. They think he killed himself. Or maybe he jumped the fence and ran for it. Nobody knows."

"Okay. He'll be the organizer if Ganzfeld asks."

When Jerry got home he emptied his overall pockets onto the table. "Pay day today." There was 11 in bills and 36 in coin."

"Did you tell them about the dead worker I saw down the road? Somebody ought to go out there and get him. He was beginning to smell."

"I did. I did," Jerry lied. "It's taken care of. They'll send a search party." He dipped his finger into the lard can and licked it.

DAVID OHLE is the author of *Motorman, The Age of Sinatra, Pisstown Chaos* and most recently *Boons & The Camp* (from which this excerpt was taken). A native of New Orleans, Ohle now lives in Lawrence, Kansas, and teaches at the University of Kansas.

About the Inside

"I'm going away by myself for a while," he said.

I was wearing a yellow ribbon in my hair. We were in the parking lot of what would appear weird to us later. The distance I wanted between us would begin in twenty minutes and was already famous.

I turned away from him and I wound up into my hair. I dropped my keys somewhere in there. I heard the bottom of my bag. It sounded like change I hadn't groped far for.

Anything can happen except when you are thinking "Anything can happen." Then you are in a line outside a theater in a parking lot complex.

When I unwound, he wasn't there.

The farther away he was from me, the more he looked like my father. He would find ways to make me more mere.

I sat by myself in the theater. What was near felt far and what was farthest was pixellated. A tiny being appeared.

"Are you kidding me, you are kidding me," the woman sitting next to me said when the concessions started singing. She was crying by the end.

It's like being in a cartoon, only it isn't really happening, was how I felt when the movie ended at the beginning of the next after.

I needed to do something new so that he would seem unfamiliar. I'd taken the yellow ribbon from a package in a store because one day when he and I were having bread, he'd forgotten to swallow. I followed his eyes to her and her eyes to where her ribbons were little slots of his thoughts.

Earlier, I had called him. "Have sandwiches with me." When he got there, they weren't sandwiches anymore. They were just bread. I had forgotten to do anything about the inside.

"You spend a lot of time alone," he said. "It makes me nervous."

"Like now?"

He tugged the ribbon I'd tied in my hair. The ribbon untied. We were in a place where people stared. I asked if he remembered the way to the way out. He said he remembered some of it. And the rest of it?

He hummed with his hand on his heart as if it was a song he'd been taught as a child to sing for the public.

"Why have you started wearing a ribbon in your hair?" he asked. When he spoke to me, he looked at other people. We were searching for something to search for. Ads for hose covered the backlit map up.

"You're too old," he said, looking at a mannequin's hair.

I tried to think about the ribboned girl and work from her toward an explanation that would include us in a plan to remember why we were.

"So you'll look at me," I said.

A woman appeared in a window to dress a mannequin. She looked at us through glossed eyes.

We were home and hardly there.

"I'm really hungry," he said, and he put his hand in my hair. I had taken out the ribbon and tied it around a handle of the dresser. The dresser wasn't important to me. It was just something that was there, like a corner. It was ugly. I felt bad having things around me that weren't important to me. A plastic colander that I'd melted. A collar from a dead dad's dog.

"Am I important to you?" I asked. Asking this was like backing into a corner.

"Sure," he said. Then he made a face that went from a frown to a smile to a different frown, only the smile wasn't a smile and neither of the frowns were frowns, and it was like something made out of plastic. If I came back much later, the face he'd made would still be there, only a little brittle.

He said, "I can't remember why I was trying to think of something sour."

"I feel like eating Thai food," he said.

I realized he was behaving in a way I had reserved for myself. He was thinking only of himself the way I thought only of me.

I tried to imagine the same thought in his brain as in my brain, how the path would snake. It would fork when we got hungry. I saw a squiggle, a string or noodle.

I made a reservation and sat there.

I was playing with my Thai food. I couldn't find a way to behave that didn't get on my nerves. My nerves were getting on my nerves.

"My stomach hurts," I said, though my stomach didn't hurt. Saying that was another way of playing with my food.

There was a small pile of string on the ground beneath our table. It led somewhere.

"Just get better," he said.

In the morning, he had a map. He showed me a place where no roads went. "This is where I'm going," he said.

I cracked an egg. Nothing came out.

"Alone?"

"Sure," he said. "I need to."

Butter hit the hot pan. The fat splattered onto his hands and burned holes in the map I could see to the floor through. Our floor was the kind laid down before we were born. It showed through to the start of something different.

He said half a word. It meant be quiet. I broke more and more eggs into the pan. The air around them burned.

He tore the map more, reaching through with his arm. It touched me where my neck was turned.

"It was old," he said.

The half he did not say was one of the most common words. It pointed to something that pointed to something that cast a shadow.

When I asked what he was thinking, most often he answered, "Thinking."

The new map showed roads where the old map showed none.

"I guess I'll have something to follow after all," he said.

When I tried to think about thinking, I saw him on the map without a road. He was trying to pitch his tent on a bright green square.

After he left, I wore the ribbon again. The farther I imagined him from me, the smaller I felt, and the smaller I felt, the larger my body seemed. I felt like a huge person tying a tiny bow as I drove the clover leaf onto the freeway.

I had been walking around in a picture. In the picture, I was small, and there was a way to move up and down levels, but I couldn't find the way.

When I saw myself in the mirror in the men's department I got out of the picture.

"Help you find anything," a man behind a man behind me said.

He pointed to a row of moving arrows. He looked like no one.

Evelyn Hampton lives in Seattle. Her website is lispservice.com.

New-Haven, Connecticut, USA
Yale University
Art + Architecture Building, Paul Rudolph Hall
M.E.D. (*Master of Environmental Design Degree*)
Credits required : 72
First Term (Fall)
714a, *Architectural Research Theories*
Credits: 3
Ljiljana Cox, B.A., B.Arch., M.A., Ph.D.

The course 714a *Method and Research* will introduce you to architectural writing and research methods, planting a background for your advanced research project (ARP). We will investigate various text genres: surveys, journalism, manifestos, scholarly essays, critical essays and narratives. A complete panorama of writing methods linked to architecture, urbanism and the environment. Today's subject: Architecture of disaster, displaying two slides. You have 3 hours left to reveal your writing skills.

Slide^number 1
Split screen
On the right, Nablus, April 3rd West Bank assault, 2002, led by the overtrained troops of the Israeli Defence Forces (IDF).
On the left, *Conical Intersect*, 1975, by Gordon Matta-Clark.

Slide^number 2
Full screen
Splitting, 1974 (photomontage), by Gordon Matta-Clark.

Appendix:

Small reminder regarding Matta-Clark (1943-1978) ———
Matta for Roberto Matta, his father (Chilean painter affiliated with the surrealist movement) and Clark for Anne Clark, his mother (artist). He studied architecture at Cornell University, then literature at the Sorbonne. It was in Paris that he became aware of the French deconstructionist philosophers and the situationists that would considerably influence his work. ———

Merle Mugwump
Course 714a

Architecture of Disaster

First, we shall parallel the slides relocated in their original frame, then from an interrogation following the 'mise en abyme' we shall establish the narrative structure of one of the possible fictions.

In 1975, Gordon Matta-Clark realized the piece entitled *Conical Intersect* for the Biennal de Paris, by cutting a large cone-shaped hole through two townhouses in the market district known as Les Halles which were to be knocked down in order to construct the then-controversial Centre Georges Pompidou. Beyond the formal aspect, this practice intended to free house spaces of their social and utilitarian constraints. The film, *Conical Intersect*, captured Matta-Clark's complex spiral cutting, which dynamically frames the construction site of the new Centre Pompidou in an impressive way.[1]

Walls open into gaps like huge portholes sprinkled with concrete junk, genuine 'overground tunnels'.[2] Matta-Clark's endoscopic anarchitecture rejects both feature and ornament. The house is no longer a house, it is lived by space, crossed by drafts. Walls become visual, physical passings, inviting investigation, rearticulating reality.

In 2002, the Israeli army launched an attack on Palestinian resistance in Nablus by cutting large cone-shaped holes through city walls located in the West Bank which was previously annihilated by the Crusaders in 1202. Beyond the formal aspect, this practice was meant to free house spaces of their visual and utilitarian constraints. The documentary images impressively captured spiral cuttings by the army complex, framing the besieged city in a compelling way.

—Question: In what measure does the theory represent a threat more real than a technological march?

A soldier, a psywarrior (Psychological Warrior), blends in with the theories of Deleuze and Guattari, Debord. If we zoom into the

[1] http://brahms.ircam.fr/works/work/20865/, *Conical Intersect* 2007 by Roque Rivas (IRCAM-Centre Pompidou)
[2] Eyal Weizman, *Hollow Land: Israel's Architecture of Occupation*, Verso, 2007

map, before the assault, in the city outskirts, the psywarrior raises his khaki shirt sleeves until he reaches the extremities of his waistcoat bullet shield and reveals his muscles. On the arms, no tattooed tribal motives, neither a stripped pin-up nor a golden eagle perched on a navy anchor, but a Dogon egg, a fresco integrating rhizomes of ginger, galanga and Jerusalem artichoke or another Go game set. *Logos* rather than a logo. We learn recently that to conceptualize the urban war led by the Israeli army against Palestinians, the Israeli military academies systematically refer to Deleuze and Guattari, in particular to *A Thousand Plateaus*, used as 'operational theory'—the used watchwords being 'Formless Rival Entities,' 'Fractal Maneuver,' 'Velocity vs. Rhythms,' 'The Wahabi War Machine,' 'Postmodern Anarchists,' 'Nomadic Terrorists'.[3] The psywarrior is keen on architecture, having studied, here, in Yale, before joining a training camp. He had already made mental series of conical breakthroughs in Paul Rudolph Hall and drifted away whole days around campus confines. Later, we find him in Nablus in the rubble of a punched-in house. The psywarrior assembles blocks of flats as concepts, he smooths the space and digs up the rhizome. He decontextualizes, he was advised in his rereadings. He devoured *On War* by Clausewitz appointing him to become hardened conceptually to fundamental principles of military strategy and to consider conflict's psychological dimension. The psywarrior is a small Prince of Prussia. He dreamed to be recruited by the Talpiot Program after Yale, he aspires to obtain the Medal of Honor.

The Talpiot Program________________________________
Talpiot program is an elite Israel Defense Forces training program inaugurated in 1979. The Talpiot program concerns young people who have demonstrated outstanding academic ability in sciences, physics and mathematics pursuing higher education prior to serving in the army. The program lasts nine years and selection is draconian. _______________

He hijacked the format to ask himself about the question of territories dividing up in their digital era. He read Blanqui attentively—*all islands or blocks belonging to barricaded streets, must be drilled in their circumference, in a way that fighters can enter and go out by the back parallel road, outside the sight and out of the enemy reach.*[4]—and as a last resort intend to pass through cellars,

[3] Mao, *On Practice and Contradiction,* (Introduced by Slavoj Zizek), Verso, 2007
[4] Auguste Blanqui, *Instructions pour une prise d'armes*, Sens & Tonka, 2000

sewers and underground, with the moles. If we have a glance at his personal library, we could believe that he is a researcher, an intellectual, a writer, an anarchist, it's one of his chameleon aspects, he made his the enemy theory. The psywarrior is a mutant soldier, he displays all basic soldier characteristics, but has integrated strong quantities of abstract toxin consistently modifying his field of vision. He infiltrates himself through walls as one crosses walls. He plots bombs, kicks away lines of strength and remodels landscapes as a perfect psychogeographer. Some of his movements could be similar to dérive. *One of the basic situationist practices is the dérive [literally: "drifting"], a technique of rapid passage through varied ambiances. Dérives involve playful-constructive behavior and awareness of psychogeographical effects, and are thus quite different from the classic notions of journey or stroll.*[5] He is a disaster architect. *Within architecture itself, the taste for dériving tends to promote all sorts of new forms of labyrinths made possible by modern techniques of construction.*[5bis] He operates a complete review. He unrolls the enemy in the middle and extirpates his vital organs. He will not go throught main streets, avenues, doors, corridors, staircases, windows. He will not be where we are waiting for him. He is too far ahead of us. He leaves wide red trails with fine pearled oxygen bubbles scattered in his passage. He brings color and leaves bodies without organs (literally without organs, nothing deleuzien here) to mark his route. He tramples fleshless opponents, crushes brains, dislocates articulations. He dispels thousands of didactics to the wind: 'We came in peace,' 'Stop fighting, surrender is good,' 'Save your family, give up,' relieved by black lacquered copters with dew-gleaming helixes. We provide you with the soundtrack that perfectly matches. High speakers censor the zone with implorations and local language screams, orders to surrender, children calling their mother. We stick you with the post-synchro that fits with your mental images. Actors were paid for it, we chose the best, the most credible, they were voice-casted. What does it feel like hearing your wife, your son, begging you to stop fighting?—because we receive non-stop mail and microfiber pop singers with our evening tray meal. The enemy is plunged into a bath of verbal 3D nightmare sequences in dolby surround. All this time, the psywarrior immerses his auditory canals into *Halloween* by John Carpenter in repeat all mode because it is revitalizing. He slides the topologically smoothed, visually vectorized plateau. He moves like a Go pawn. He plays with

[5] *Internationale situationniste number 2, Théorie de la dérive*, décembre 1958
[5bis] Op.Cit.

black pawns, the enemy does not even play against him, it is not really necessary to hold him informed. He did not grasp at once the reason why his trainer came down the first day with a Go game set and said: 'Here is your battle zone' or how to cross some combinatorial abstracted game of strategy with live action ground. Afterward that makes him laugh out loud. *Go works distributing itself through the space, taking the space, keeping the possibility to appear at any point. The movement does not go from one point to another, but is perpetual, without boundaries, without aim or destination, without departure or arrival [...] It proceeds altogether differently, territorializing or deterritorializing it (make the outside a territory in space, consolidate that territory by construction of a second, adjacent territory).*[6] To be a pawn is not an insult any more, it's a mental projection. Upon the goban, houses are so many compartments to be kicked away on which we "strike" stone-soldiers. Two boots by compartment is the rule. The pawn is always covered in offensive toys. We created him a special wartoy perfecting his outfit, the Moleskin^WEAPON TM. We accessorized him, and the other go pawn rhizomatically connected. Moleskin^WEAPON TM is a kind of completed mini ram to kick down concrete walls. This name comes from *Condylura cristata*, a small North American mole with a tentacular snout endowed with a multitude of electromagnetic senso-sensors. The Moleskin^WEAPON TM is not the only psywarrior reference to the animal kingdom. *Although several thousand soldiers and Palestinian guerrillas were manoeuvring simultaneously in the city, they were so 'saturated' into the urban fabric that very few would have been visible from the air.. [...] they moved horizontally through walls and vertically throughholes blasted in ceilings and floors. This form of movement, described by the military as 'infestation,' seeks to redefine inside as outside, and domestic interiors as thoroughfares.*[7] All concepts are good if they inspire new modes of action. Theory is psywarrior's fuel oil. He moves into his bubble, the reversible (black&white) pawn soldier armed with his so practical Moleskin^WEAPON TM. He drills walls, grounds, he draws his road. He gets closer, maybe he is there, behind you, still masked by the

[6] Gilles Deleuze & Félix Guattari, *A Thousand Plateaus: Capitalism and Schizophrenia*, University of Minnesota Press, 1987

[7] Eyal Weizman, *Hollow Land: Israel's Architecture of Occupation*, Verso, 2007

& further inspiration from:

* Carl Schmitt, *La guerre civile mondiale*, éditions è®e, 2007—Bulletin of Yale University, School of Architecture,
2008-2009, august 2008—Jacob von Uexküll, *Mondes animaux et monde humain*, Denoël, 1965
http://psywarrior.com — http://psywar.org/.
Wandering Souls, performance by Sandy Amerio & Patrick Bouvet, 2008

smooth concrete thickness. He is going to extract your core boring life as a perfect brazilophile (concrete/paint/air/couch/fabric/flesh/air/tv screen /paint /concrete) and so on and so on.

—translated by Laure Motet & Monica Karski

Émilie Notéris was born in 1978. She's a French writer and member of a literary review called *TINA* (There is No Alternative—Literature). Her first book *Cosmic Trip* was published in 2008 (éditions IMHO) and she co-directed an essay with Jérôme Schmidt 'J.G. Ballard, Hautes Altitudes' (éditions è®e, 2008).

Dakota

The assignment was to express your personality through one of the fifty states, to pick one out that described your proclivities and ailments. There were no rules or real suggestions about how to choose. The teacher—who was not American but not so un-American as to make us think too hard—told us to 'follow our guts.' Some people chose states they were born in, or states whose shapes reminded them of something about themselves—the 'boot,' the 'square,' and so on. My state was Dakota: It had that uninterested, rocky ring to it. Our teacher, who was in her later fifties, never forced me to specify North or South, and that was fine with me. Badlands or Great Plains, the choice was impossible.

Each student had to give a presentation. I made a poster and drew big ice-cubes on it. Inside each ice-cube I wrote a word that described me: single, smart, natural, instinctual, thinker. I colored in the space around the ice-cubes with a brown magic marker. When I made my presentation I told them the brown areas represented root beer, and the ice-cubes represented aspects of my personality. "I don't know what it means," I said. I told them how I felt being alive was a messy, hot disgusting way to be. "I sweat so much in my sleep I wake up three, four times a night and put down more and more towels. Winter, spring, summer, fall, it makes no difference."

I looked up Dakota in the dictionary and learned it meant 'allies' in some other language. I told my classmates they were my 'allies.' "The idea behind my state is that if we work together to get along, we won't butt heads. But not butting heads is all we'll do together. It's all we'll ever aim to do." It made sense to me for a moment.

Our class was held in a low-ceilinged conference hall in the basement of an unmarked municipal building. The security guards were two versions of man I tend to disrespect: the jack-hammermouthed, blue-eyed joker and the fat and lazy weepy kind. In order to gain access to the building we had to answer certain questions correctly. The one of them I always stalled on was, "How's it hanging?"

When I wasn't in class, I was building up a spherical knowledge of the city. It was a city whose downtown was central and whose peripheries were defined by a ring of suburban streets outside of which were just big highways shooting out like fingers on a hand. Underneath it all was a backwashy body of water sloshing around. I rode the elevated train that made stops around the suburbs in a hoop. If I wanted to go downtown I just looked out the window as I circled around and changed my mind.

I had an apartment in an area called "The Thralls," in one of the new highrises that lured prospective tenants with catchy names like "The Queen Mary" or like "Decorum Towers." I lived in the "Côte des Miroirs" in a second-story one-bedroom. From the outside it looked like the kind of building home to dental offices or some other kind of office wherein exacting measures were taken against decay. Or so I liked to think—that time spent at home would be cleansing, filling, improving something. It was a ten-story stucco thing with a short walk up to a glass door that opened automatically, as if the building could see you, or sense you, and didn't want you to touch it. The foyer was paved in blood-colored vinyl. In the elevator was a single line of vandalism: "I feel like a Vampire," written small in black permanent marker on the white, polycarbonate ceiling.

Besides these details, the interior was a beige-and-eggshell situation with chrome sconces, a blond wood panel here and there. I felt at peace in the halls and foyer. I liked it there. My apartment itself was minutely furnished and dull. Mostly I read class hand-outs, cookbooks, tabloids on the lush seafoam sofa in the foyer, or seated Indian-style on the freshly vacuumed carpeted hallway outside my door.

One day our teacher started us on a week-long learning module. We worked in teams. "Couples," the teacher called it. I was paired up with a girl whose name I wasn't allowed to know. We got two chairs and placed them face-to-face and sat down. My legs crossed themselves uncomfortably. "When I come around I'm going to whisper something in your ear," our teacher said. "Your job is to act out what I tell you without letting on to the other person that you know what you're doing." The girl was someone I'd noticed in the class but had cast off by the second day as young and uncurious and married—dirty blond hair cut short, sleeveless collared shirts, knee-length skirts which looked more like hospital wear on her kind of flat, wide, unprotrudishing body. No florals of any kind. Not my type

We were among the last to get whispered to. Around the room people were pretending to drive cars, gnashing out drunk slurs of blame, or screaming about stolen money. A younger male student yelled out, "You're lying—my father is not in the hospital," and an older woman asked her partner—a tall boy who lit a cigarette while he listened—"For the last time, where is the invaluable ancient relic? Your secrecy puts us both in grave danger." When the teacher got to us she whispered something in the girl's ear and to me she pulled out a type-written index card and read it out loud, unfairly it seemed, so we could both hear: "Dakota. You tend to murder women. Look at the young lady across from you. Make her feel you're in love with her because you love her thoughts and feelings. Even her terror, whatever she has inside."

The girl, my partner, ended up staying at my place for the week, mostly talking and eyeing me across the desk—which I used as a kitchen table, bedside table, and desk—as she told exhaustive stories of the demise of her parents' lukewarm romance, then shorter blurbs about her highschool friends, her trip to Europe. When she got hungry I put out a loaf of raisin bread. She undid the twisty tie and let a slice flop around her face until she stuffed it into her mouth, whole.

I decided before the whole thing began that my method of seduction would be one of ignorance and denial of interest. I'd seen that work in movies. The first day I asked the girl pat questions—what her skills are, her experiences, her goals—and then I just sat and stared and thought about my own face—what it felt like hanging off my skull. My nods were less nods than sighs, which I tried to make totally objectively: just exhaling more air than usual. Her voice was piquant, solicitous, but I kept remembering myself, my face, my breath, and I survived.

The second day my mood evened out a bit. I listened and didn't listen to her words and coughs and chair creak. I started to feel sort of blissful, unrepugnant of time, awash in something. I imagined my face to be like a bright open sky and my thoughts like clouds drifting past my eyes in different shapes: a house, an axe, a giraffe, a baby. It seemed to have an intoxicating effect on the girl. A bit of color appeared on her cheeks.

Several times during her long, trauma-ed speeches she looked at me as though to say, "just a little longer until I let you touch me," and I'd actually feel something like love between us—a little flash of lightning. And then all at once, passing in the living room to and from the toilet we kissed in a manner much like the slice of bread: roving benignly around our mouths and then suddenly and completely consumed.

So it went on like that for a few more days—stretches of blanketed half-awareness marked with short ecstasies of correctly-placed guesses of where she and I might have things in common.

Saturday night she went home "for a change of clothes" and never came back.

Monday she walked into class with her hair reshortened, less sensible shoes on. And didn't look my way or say a word. The teacher sat each of us down in two-minute conferences and asked us what had happened. She called the girl over first: "Miss Issippi," is how she identified her.

Grades were recorded under assignment title and posted on the bulletin board outside the men's restroom: "Selfish People: B minus."

I suffered for weeks afterwards with what I came to term as 'morning sickness.' It was a feeling upon waking, a kind of unjustified, sourceless pain throughout my body that made me want to die. It took a gross amount of caffeine and some ugly calisthenics for me to have the courage to present myself to the world again. It was my intention, during all of this time, to hone my skills of survival as a soldier, retaining the elegance and self-righteousness of a diplomat or of a lawyer or some other successful type of man. I wore suits and parted my hair those days. I checked my breath in the only way that one can get a truly accurate assessment of what his mouth smells like: I licked the back of my hand.

Before we could graduate we had a few weeks of training out in the field. What we were preparing to do, what this whole thing was supposed to culminate in for us, was to become a person who neither catches criminals nor stands idly by, but an individual who intrudes, gets involved as an actor in situations of gravity with little or no effect. We had to learn how not to be victimized, how to assume roles, how to encourage—in the most literal sense of the word—good people to let bad things happen to them.

"Except your fate," the teacher wrote on the board in carefully rounded cursive. I just barely understood what she was getting at.

My assignment was to show up in a truck—color, make, model and year unspecified—on a particular stretch of highway at dusk. There was to be an accident. The teacher said my role and purpose would be obvious. Because I was driving a truck, I could put something like a big axe—the kind a lumberjack would use—in the bed of it. When I got there, exactly on time, I knew to trust my instincts. I dragged the bleeding man from his car on to the gravel on the side of the road and got my axe out. "What the hell are you doing?" he cried. His arms and legs hung and swayed awkwardly as he writhed. "Keep still," I said. I swung at him repeatedly, each time just missing a piece of his body and wedging the blade of the axe into the dry dirt. "You're delirious," I told him. "An ambulance is coming. Don't you worry!" and I swung again.

Miss Issippi drives a periwinkle sedan. She has several hologramatic stickers on her bumper. The car locks and unlocks by pressing a button she keeps on her keychain. Her keychain has a lot of keys on it. She keeps all these keys on it because it makes her feel important. She sings along to songs on the radio because it makes her feel like a star. She talks to herself in a baby voice. There are old French fries on the floor of her back seat. There are old newspapers still in the blue plastic bag the delivery boy uses when it's raining. The old French fries taste like Miss Issippi's armpits. I hold them in my bottom lip all day. If that makes me look like a gorilla then so be it. So be it.

I want to tell you something that will change your life. You know that stranger that keeps appearing over and over on the street, on the corner, pretending to be on his merry way? Sooner or later he'll have you alone somewhere. And he's going to want one thing: to drain all the life out of you. And what he'll say is that he's been watching you, that he knows you, that there's nothing you can do or say to keep him from you, and you'll see the passion in his eyes and for a second you'll feel a little proud and special for being singled-out by this man. As he paces the room, edging ever closer to where you are huddled over by the window you will consider your options. Be killed by this man or jump to your own death. Maybe the day will be a cloudy one and somehow that will fluff up your perception of what hitting pavement might feel like. You're wasting time with that imagination of yours. In this situation there is only one solution. Bash your head against the wall. Remove your clothes and tie them around your neck. Pray for the man to help you tie the knots tighter. Ask him to chew on your face. Beg him, crying, to procure a knife suitable for your own decapitation. Tell him you've been waiting for this moment all your life. Tell him, "I love you." And scream and writhe on the floor.

Ottessa Moshfegh lives in Providence, Rhode Island. Her stories have appeared in *Fence, NOON* and *Unsaid.*

Had I not journeyed to Malta in May of 2007, the book you now hold in your hands could never have existed. Had I not fallen in the shadows of the Co-Cathedral of St John in Valletta and broken my ankle, my departure for London would not have been delayed and I would not have found myself, less than a week later, a point of contestation between the American embassy and a group of aged former conspirators eager to keep their activities in the years prior to independence as hidden as they had been for more than forty years. (See my memoir *A Death by the Sea.*) I almost certainly would not have visited the [------------------------] and discovered in its stuffy library a box containing papers written by Samuel Taylor Coleridge during his months in Malta two centuries ago, papers left behind upon his departure and apparently never referenced again. As astounding as that discovery was—the essentially complete text of a hitherto unknown narrative poem of some five hundred lines, along with memoiristic materials of a no less surprising nature (See the compendium I call *Disbelief*)—that which is detailed in the following pages is more remarkable still: a continuation and completion of the unfinished Gothic poem "Christabel," begun by Coleridge in 1797, extended in 1800 and published in 1816 without these pages which were composed in Malta and, like the texts of *Disbelief*, left behind in 1805. Coleridge's dismissal of these exotic and dramatic writings—nay, his apparent amnesia regarding them—can only be taken as further proof of the profound psychological breakdown the poet experienced in Malta, a breakdown which may not have substantially redirected the course of the remainder of his life but certainly deepened and intensified already prominent characteristics: a well-established sense of self-pity, an almost total inability to resume the production of poetry (outside of Malta, that is), and a safe harbouring in significantly more "conservative" thought, particularly in a religious sense.

"Christabel" is itself both culmination and harbinger. While "The Rime of the Ancient Mariner" operates out of an apparently Catholic milieu, its heart lies in the conversion of the mariner, a rather stereotypically Protestant experience. The most sensationalist and supernatural elements—the most ungodly, we might suggest—precede the conversion: the worldly life gives way to the heavenly. "Christabel," on the other hand, is almost perforce Catholic, owing to its medieval setting: the diabolically supernatural and the godly exist spatially and temporally side by side in a way that tends to make "mainline" Protestants uncomfortable. Coleridge himself never converted to Catholicism—had he done so he might now be regarded as a precursor of the later Tractarians—but his retreat (mirrored by Wordsworth's) into highly traditional thought-forms almost presupposes, at least for an imagination such as Coleridge's, a deliberate, if conscious, search for shelter from horror.

But what was the horror? Was it his imagination itself? Was he too capable of imagining his fantasies to be real? Or had he come to believe for whatever reason in the then traditionalist (now fundamentalist) fires of hell? Did he have an epiphany about his laudanum addiction (which, in any case, he never conquered)? Or did something happen to him in Malta? Did his months there, in one of the world's most profoundly Roman Catholic countries and among a people so long subjected to foreign overlords, open his eyes to reality in a way rationalist England could not?

"Christabel" cannot, of course, answer these questions: it is a work of poetic fiction set in a stridently non-rational time and place. But the mood of this hitherto unknown conclusion certainly reflects Coleridge's state of mind during its composition in Malta. Would that preparing the poem for publication and discussing its merits and demerits had remained so simple!

It did not.

First, there is the matter of the text itself. While it is clearly a completion of "Christabel," it is less clearly *Coleridge's* completion of the poem. The pages themselves—unlike the materials I previously edited for *Disbelief*—do not exist in Coleridge's own hand. In fact they do not exist in Coleridge's own words. What I have discovered, most unusually, is a Maltese translation of the three concluding parts of the poem. (Maltí is a Semitic language, presumably dating back to Phoenician times.) The translation maintains the four-stress line of Coleridge's original—that is, the same tetrameter as the first two parts of "Christabel"—but eschews any attempt at rhyme. It is, however, so close in sense to the unknown original that, as I began to translate back into English, rhymes almost fell into my lap. For this reason what you will read in the upcoming pages is, I feel, remarkably close to the text first penned in English, with the caveat of course that I am merely a translator and not one of the English language's most esteemed poets. There will undoubtedly be lines, rhymes and rhythms which you will find infelicitous, but with which I have done my best. Would that preparing the poem for publication had remained so simple!

It did not.

For, in the second place, it is not in fact indubitable that the anonymous Maltese translator (the CR of *Disbelief*?) was translating words that Coleridge wrote. There is no question that parts 3-5, included here, are built upon the uncontested work of Coleridge in parts one and two, nor can one blithely dismiss the faith (one might say) in the authorship of these pages indicated by the monks who placed it with the "Lykos" materials of *Disbelief*. And even though Coleridge waited more than a decade after his time in Malta to publish parts one and two and, when doing so, stated categorically that he *yet intended to finish* the poem published incomplete, these actions are not inconsistent with the breakdown of 1804-05. By 1816, when John Murray brought out the small volume which also included "Kubla Khan," there was still another work more than a decade in the past, though it had already been published quite successfully: Walter Scott's *The Lay of the Last Minstrel*, a poem at the very least inspired by Scott's having heard a recitation of the fragmentary "Christabel." Coleridge, in fact, felt it necessary to establish in his introduction to the 1816 volume the dates of "Christabel"'s composition, in order to protect himself from the charge of having stolen from Scott. Lord Byron brought the publication about, prodding both Coleridge to release his unfinished work and Murray to produce the volume. (Though accounts remain inconclusive to this day, I have little doubt that the duel fought by Lord Byron and then Sir Walter Scott in Missalonghi, Greece, in 1824 was occasioned at least in part by Byron's championing Coleridge at Scott's expense. The Greek engraving which accompanied initial reports of Byron's beheading of Scott is as gruesome and, in some ways, delightful as the work of Goya and remains too little seen by those who read only English.)

But 1816 is notable for still more than the rounding out of Coleridge's poetic canon and is a prominent date for those to whom Coleridge is simply an albatross around the neck. 1816 is also the year of the horrid night or horrid dare, in which Lord Byron, Percy Bysshe Shelley, Mary

Shelley and Dr John Polidori (Byron's attendant) strove to outdo one another in composing the most frightening tale. Both Mary Shelley's *Frankenstein* and Polidori's "The Vampyre" grew out of this night. Polidori's brief work—apparently based on an idea of Byron's—first saw magazine publication anonymously and was at the outset taken to be Byron's work. Byron subsequently published "Augustus Darvell" (or "Fragment of a Novel") as evidence that "The Vampyre" was not his. But the nexus is evocative: Polidori, eager to work on avowedly Gothic material, clever enough to write but perhaps less gifted at ideation; Byron, whose prodigious memory for recitation had already helped disseminate knowledge of Coleridge's work; and Coleridge, publishing the incomplete poem which very few can have believed him likely to finish. By 1819 when Sherwood, Neely & Jones published The *Vampyre* in book form, three more years had elapsed in which Coleridge had done nothing with "Christabel" despite this statement: "I trust that I shall be able to embody in verse the three parts yet to come, in the course of the present year." Polidori, meanwhile, had a flair for the outré and an ability to expand upon pre-existing ideas.

So what? you may well ask. If Polidori was so enamoured of Coleridge's work and had the ear of a publisher, why did he not release the work? One, Coleridge was still alive and not likely to assent; two, Polidori himself was dead within two years. The question then becomes, Might Polidori have finished the poem, holding onto it (or turning it over to Murray) in the expectation of the notoriously unhealthy Coleridge's imminent demise? If so, the text did not come to light when Polidori died in 1821, nor has it shown up in the Murray family papers. Instead it has surfaced only now, in Maltí, in a cabinet with other Coleridge materials. Case closed, no?

No. Because John Polidori betook himself to Malta in 1820, ostensibly to serve as doctor to the British governor, but actually, I suspect, with an eye toward getting his hands on the Coleridge material, about which rumours may have been floating: Remember that Coleridge was provocatively verbose when under the influence of laudanum. If such rumours existed, they were not recorded—at least not in any materials subsequently published or catalogued—but this circumstance may not be as discouraging as it seems. Coleridge's admirers were protective of their demi-god and would have seen little value in recording for posterity delusions which served primarily to emphasize his inability to compose any significant verse. Furthermore, the broader nature of any ravings about Malta (Again I refer you to *Disbelief*) would have conclusively dampened any desire to investigate Coleridge's time there.

But Polidori—surely his time in Malta will have been discussed at length in the various critical approaches to his work? Surely not. Critics generally see only two reasons to mention Polidori at all—one, his service to Byron; and two, his authorship of "The Vampyre." In the first case, he is not a personality in his own right, but rather merely a reflection; in the second, he is chiefly an embarrassment, a reminder that—despite the critical esteem given to *Frankenstein* and "The Turn of the Screw"—the literary establishment would rather forget that "horror" fiction exists and was not scorned in the past by authors who ought to have known better. That "Christabel" and "The Rime of the Ancient Mariner" still merit anthologization owes less to the undeniable quality of their writing than to their sociological import: "Christabel" as an investigation of female sexuality and "The Rime" as a prime mover in the Romantic movement. In fact the former—the terribly freighted feminine sensuality of "Christabel"—is one of the major pointers to the possibility, if not probability, that Polidori rather than Coleridge finished the poem. For the very feminine nature of the desire in parts one and two of the poem—a desire not irrefutably not lesbian—shifts quite abruptly in these "new" sections. The shift operates in two ways, only one of which the earlier parts foreshadow—that is, Geraldine's seduction of Sir Leoline. The second thread of this new emphasis is, however, entirely novel: while Coleridge focused his implication and innuendo on the desire stirred by or within the two female characters, the later focus is Sir Leoline, whose lust is handled quite openly. If Coleridge penned these parts, both re-emphasis and frankness must be part and parcel of his breakdown, the result of the same almost unrestrained fervor that produced the verses of "Son of Lykos" and the extraordinary memoir which companions them in the Maltese cabinet. So interpreted, they represent an astonishing breakthrough for Coleridge, a melding—one might say—of his innermost self as revealed in his journals with his rather more decorous public persona, but such an exhibition is so inexplicable outside his breakdown and its attendant psychosis that he was incapable of acknowledging the new writing or ever returning to it to prepare it for publication.

If, on the other hand, Polidori wrote this conclusion, then the shifts of tone and emphasis—and they are substantial—betray not only the differences in the mental states of "Christabel"'s two authors, but also the impact upon Polidori of Byron's profligate lifestyle and the publication of the initial cantos of *Don Juan*. Furthermore, the male orientation of the lust in the new conclusion to "Christabel" is entirely consistent with the masculine (and even homo-erotic) elements of "The Vampyre."

Parts three through five of "Christabel" likewise reveal a novelistic approach to plotting and dialogue, which one is tempted to see as a Polidorian characteristic. Such an argument remains inconclusive because "Son of Lykos" exhibits the same traits. The rather languid and haunted air of the two-part "Christabel" gives way to a more frenetic, but still haunted, level of activity. The broken rhythms which feel so "modern" might point either to Polidori's relative lack of skill as a poet or to Coleridge's disturbed state of mind. The details concerning the "black magic" of Geraldine and the hermit's spiritual powers in resistance arguably reflect both the Italian Catholicism of Polidori's background and the Maltese Catholicism into which Coleridge was immersed once he arrived on the island. (It is interesting too how readily this aspect of the poem foreshadows many elements of post-Tolkien "adult fantasy." Tolkien, not coincidentally, was Catholic.)

If we had the original English text, a linguistic analysis of vocabulary and syntax could point us toward a near-certain identification of the author, even granting that Polidori was deliberately assuming the role of another writer. An analysis of this translation must of course be less certain, as the words before us approach at a double remove, having passed through the hands of two translators to reach us. It may never be possible to state with any degree of assurance who wrote these lines. Whether they are an acceptable conclusion to "Christabel," whoever wrote them, is a decision I defer to the individual reader.

—Valletta, Malta, July 24, 2009

Cooper Renner is the author of *Mosefolket* and the translator of Mario Bellatin's *Chinese Checkers*. He has had poems recently in *Unsaid* and *Keyhole*. Other parts of the Maltese material have appeared, or will appear, in *New York Tyrant*, *Keyhole* and *Anemone Sidecar*.

An Invitation

A dun-colored cab came slyly out of the fog and up the drive, steaming in a way alive. Ned neared with a thuggish duffel bag and the trunk popped up, and the driver emerged, a shapeless man—two eyes, a nose, somewhere a mouth—a common creature, distinctive as a carrot, gone hairy, limply aged. He fit the occasion, self described as from the County that northern blank, seeming flat but for Khattadin on the map. Fog was as nothing to a man from Aroostook used to much worse; whereas Nick, Nick was from a softer part of the country and bound for an even softer place: Bermuda of the pretty clichés—pink sands, turquoise waters. Phoebe had said hurricane season is best for lots of reasons.

Blank

I remember finding tooth whitener in her medicine cabinet; it was packaged like narcotics. The vials didn't have an expiration date. They were toxic, I'm sure. Ned felt the phlegmy latch of complaint he coughed up all too frequently rise in his throat.

Shouldn't he be finished talking about the family romance?

Of course not! like a stern housekeeper, knock, knock, knocking an iron against a shirt, banged against and scorching the shirt, never once looking up at Ned, Dr. K said, Of course not! For a time then, Ned talked about William Maxwell, whose mother had died in the influenza epidemic of 1918, when the writer was still a boy. Maxwell and the background on Maxwell was a part of the throat-clearing. The novel Ned was thinking of was as much a memoir as novel. *So Long, See You Tomorrow*—He loved the promise of that title, its sweet, melancholy expectation of ongoing time together, a promise overturned in an instant. "After…there were no more disasters." That's what Maxwell said…wrote…says, oh, how can he be so fucking certain that the worst has happened?

Ned stared at a filing cabinet, as attractive as an air conditioner—a box with handles—hardly soothing. He coughed. He did the hitching trick with his throat to clear it more vehemently. I never really looked at your furniture before. Like the bookcase in the waiting room, Ned said. Where did that come from?

Where do you think it came from?

A lake house, that's where the bookcase came from. A wet place that never dried out, a slime-colored cube entered unwillingly though the lake itself was invitingly velvety.

I know I'm talking about cunt, Ned said, and he reviled the attic-eclectic interior of Dr. K's waiting room. The glass-fronted bookcase, in its black, cracked veneer, a wood leached of light as if the bookcase had been drowned, recovered, used in the lake house for cook books and jelly jars—one full of pennies—the glass-fronted bookcase housed a set of cloth books, water-marked and faded. To the doctor's credit there were no Hieronymus Bosch prints, no ghastly garden of earthly delights.

You make me more hateful than I am, Ned said, by way of good-bye, then shut the door. Hardly polite, hardly charming.

Hardly the way you were at the bar is what the woman last night had said with her pudendum in his face.

Poor snake.

Ned walked down York, turned west onto something ugly. The street should have been beautiful—not this mottled, uneven, narrow way all the way to a greater contraction, an underground entrance dank as the boathouse; subway stink and the usual terrors near the tracks before the train, and then he was on it—in it, a box that shunted downtown and made him faintly sick. Your money or your life.

He once knew a girl with a crooked face—who was she? What did her eyebrows do?

Sometimes when he came home, he loved his wife acutely.

Isabel?

The experience of calling after someone is an experience he no longer wants to have. He is broke; there wasn't so much money after all. Poor Pet and her vials of teeth bleach.

Mother!

He was forty-two. The fellowship that had funded him through Fife and London and Rome and Lime House was long since spent, so, too, his talents for attaching to comfortable people. Exhausting. How he had limped along, an adjunct, until with Stahl's help he turned associate-something. He should have been a vet. Really.

Isabel said. Your thoughts are so depressingly obvious.

You'll have to tell me because I don't know what it is I'm thinking.

CHRISTINE SCHUTT is the author of two short-story collections and *Florida*, a novel and National Book Award finalist. Her second novel, *All Souls*, was a finalist for the 2009 Pulitzer Prize in fiction. Schutt is a senior editor of the literary annual *NOON*. She lives and teaches in New York City.

from An Introduction to the Work of Ivan Menchov
by Igor Lenchov

Prefatory Note: I first became acquainted with Menchov while lecturing in the department of Applied Linguistics at National University. Menchov was the Department Chair. It was my honor to assist Menchov on the project that would eventually produce the groundbreaking *repertory linguistic method.*
—Igor Lenchov

Menchov the Mentor

You have to strike the right tone, Menchov said, you have to hit the right note, he said. Strike the right note and it all comes down, Menchov said to me. It's like a hill of bricks or a box of rocks, Menchov said. It's like a house of cards, he said, snapping his fingers. Pick the right card and it all comes down, said Menchov. Every word is a stone and every stone is a piece, he said, every word a stony piece in a stony pile, said Menchov. Knock it down, Menchov said, pointing at me. I can't, I said to Menchov, I can't do it, I said. Yes, you can, Menchov said. See the hill of stones, hear the mound of sounds, said Menchov. Knock them down, he said, pointing at me, nodding his head. Everything I say is made of sand, Menchov said, ruin my dune, he said, nodding at me. How, I said, how can I do it, I said, shaking my head. Use the method, Menchov said, use the repertory linguistic method, he said. I'll try, I said to Menchov, nodding at Menchov. I have to hit the right tone, I said, I have to strike the right note. That's right, Menchov said, go on, he said. I have to kick the bricks, I said, lifting my voice, I have to knock the box of rocks, I said. Yes, Menchov said, go on, he said. I have to pound the mound of sound, I said, I have to fall the wall down, I said. Yes, Menchov said, that's right, said Menchov. I have to crack the stack, I said, shouting at Menchov, I have to ruin the dune, I said, raising my fists at Menchov. I have to ruin you, I said, screaming at Menchov. Yes, Menchov said, smiling at me, now you have it, he said.

Menchov's Vision

Everything is permitted, Menchov said, pouring the wine. Phonologically, everything is possible, said Menchov. Breath becomes death, guns become nuns, swans become swine, Menchov said, sniffing his wine. Do not be surprised, Menchov said, when nights become naughts, suns become moons, nihilists become stylists, said Menchov, lifting his glass, clinking his glass against mine. Producers become seducers, Menchov said, shrugging his shoulders. Do not fear the morphophonemic, Menchov said, the cups and pucks, the gods and the dogs, said Menchov, drinking his wine. Everything is permitted, Menchov said, kissers become killers, mothers become lovers, blond men turn blind, said Menchov, gulping his wine. Murmurers become murderers, said Menchov, waving his hand. I have heard the phonemes laughing in the night, Menchov said, pouring the wine. I have heard schwas yawning at dawn, said Menchov, drinking his wine. People will tell you the ant is not related to the elephant, Menchov said, they will deny the bee in the wildebeest, he said, but what do they know, said Menchov. You and I, my dear Lenchov, said Menchov, we will show the world the possibilities, Menchov said. We will show the world the phonological possibilities, so Menchov said.

Menchov Recycles

Ah, Menchov said, here are my clothes, said Menchov, pointing at the clothes on his desk. Here are my cycling clothes, said Menchov, pulling on his wool cycling shorts. Why are you wearing cycling clothes, I said to Menchov, taking a bite of my donut. I will tell you, Menchov said, I will tell you in just one minute, said Menchov, pulling on his wool cycling shirt. You see, Menchov said, my nephew is growing up, he said, my nephew has outgrown his tricycle, said Menchov. I see, I said, your nephew is getting to be a big boy, I said. Yes, Menchov said, and he has asked for a favor, said Menchov, my nephew has asked me to help him recycle his tricycle, said Menchov, pulling on his cycling socks. Ah, I said, that's very sensible, to recycle the tricycle, I said. Yes, Menchov said, but it will not be easy, said Menchov, I must ride my bicycle to recycle the tricycle, said Menchov. I forgot your nephew's name, I said, what is his name again, I said. Michael, Menchov said, his name is Michael but everyone calls him Mike, said Menchov. Good for Mike, I said, good for Mike to recycle his trike, I said. Wait a minute, Menchov said, just a minute, said Menchov, I'm the one recycling the tricycle, he said, I'm the one riding the bicycle to recycle Mike's tricycle, said Menchov. Mike is a sensible boy, I said, nodding my head, a very sensible boy, I said. Yes, Menchov said, but don't forget I'm the one riding the bike to recycle Mike's trike, Menchov said. I would like to meet Mike, I said, I would like to shake Mike's hand, I said, I would like to commend Michael, I said. Fuck that, Menchov said, taking off his wool biking shirt, I'm not riding my bike to recycle Mike's trike, he said, taking off his wool biking shorts. I'm not riding my bicycle to recycle Michael's tricycle, said Menchov, throwing the trike in the trash.

Menchov's Dog

Hundreds are dead, Menchov said, reading the newspaper. Hundreds have died in the disaster, said Menchov. Many who are still alive, Menchov said, reading the newspaper, many of the so-called survivors have injuries of which they will no doubt die, said Menchov, passing the newspaper to me. God help them, I said, reading the newspaper. Yes, Menchov said, summoning his dog from the corner of the laboratory, snapping his fingers at his borzoi. Do you think god will help them, Menchov said, petting his dog. Do you think god will help these so-called survivors, Menchov said. I don't know, I said. If god exists, then I suppose he will help these so-called survivors, I said. And you, I said, what do you think, I said to Menchov, Menchov petting his borzoi. It is a phonological situation, Menchov said, for me it is a phonological matter, he said, scratching his dog's ears. If they believe in god they will live, but if they deny god they will die, said Menchov. Interesting, I said, believe and live, deny and die, I said. Yes, Menchov said, rubbing his dog's belly. It makes phonological sense, I thought, we should apply the method to this theory, I thought. We should apply the repertory linguistic method to your theory, I said to Menchov. That's what I was thinking, Menchov said, sending his dog to the corner, sending his dog away.

Menchov in Love

All my lovers asked about my mother, Menchov said. Every lover I ever took asked about my mother, said Menchov. Year after year, lover after lover, asking about my mother, Menchov said. But you never knew your mother, I said to Menchov. That's right, Menchov said, I never knew her, he said. And then I took a lover who never asked about my mother, said Menchov, I loved this lover unlike any other, said Menchov. I loved this lover who never asked about my mother, said Menchov. This lover became my wife, Menchov said, my terrible wife, said Menchov. Your terrible wife never asked about your mother, I said. No, Menchov said, and I will tell you why, said Menchov. My terrible wife is my mother, Menchov said, she is the one and the other, so Menchov said. Your lover is your mother, I said. Don't tell anyone, Menchov said, putting his finger over his lips. That's taboo, I said, your mother cannot be your lover, I said. Ah, Menchov said, everything is permitted, said Menchov, smiling at me. Everything is permitted phonologically, he said.

Menchov on Ice

This is very cold, Menchov said, this ice is very cold, he said, holding the ice in his hand. This ice is frozen, Menchov said. Yes, I said, it just came from the freezer, I said, I just took it out of the deep freeze, I said. Oh, Menchov said, it is so very cold, he said, pressing the ice to his cheek. The ice is freezing my face, Menchov said, holding the ice to his cheek. What is wrong, I said, what is wrong with your face, I said. Nothing, Menchov said, pressing the ice to his nose. It tickles, Menchov said, holding the ice to his nose, the ice is so cold it tickles, said Menchov, giggling from the ice. It's melting just a little bit, Menchov said, pointing at the drops on his chin. It's turning into water, Menchov said. Yes, I said, it's melting, I said. This is the coldest ice I've ever held, Menchov said, slipping the ice down his pants. Ah, Menchov said, the ice is so very cold, he said, squirming in his chair. It hurts, Menchov said, cupping his crotch. The ice hurts my balls, said Menchov. You should not have put it in your pants, I said, shaking my head. It's freezing my balls, Menchov said, cupping his crotch. Help me, Menchov said, help, said Menchov. I don't know why you put ice in your pants, I said to Menchov, reaching my hand in his pants.

Menchov's End

I am going to kill Menchov, I said to myself, I am going to kill him, I thought, walking to the cake table. I am going to murder him, I thought, picking up the cake knife. What's that you say, Menchov said, taking a bite of cake. I can't hear you, Menchov said, you're murmuring, he said. I am going to kill you, I thought, looking at Menchov. Open your mouth when you speak, Menchov said to me, what is wrong with you, he said, taking a sip of punch. I am going to kill, I thought, holding the cake knife. You are murmuring, Menchov said, I can't hear you, said Menchov, eating his cake. I am going to kill Menchov, I thought. You're murmuring, Menchov said, you're a murmurer, said Menchov, murmurer!

M. T. FALLON lives in Colorado. Recent fiction in *Abjective, Avatar Review, New York Tyrant* and *Unsaid.*

Thirteen Shapes

So I came by, and you weren't around. "Gone to pasture," read the note stuck to the door with gum. I took it to mean you were dining out and so waited for as long as it took to sing the twenty-one songs of our youth. After which, I went to fetch a drink of water. When I returned, the note had changed to one I couldn't make out. It was, perhaps, a geometric message, for there were thirteen distinct shapes crowded onto the page in some sort of relationship to each other. The gum was fresh and smelled of cinnamon—your favorite. I peeked through the window. Inside, the thirteen shapes had grown dimensions and concealed the room in a tangle, but I could tell you were there because of the cat.

Tubes

The end of the tube, flitting about like a hummingbird, discharges a yellowish oatmeal, which seals the ear. After finishing with the other ear, the tube is lifted up and away. This is not the finger of some factory robot, filling ears on an assembly line, as one might expect, but rather an independent creature with a reproductive cycle, the yellowish oatmeal a form of egg foam. Long ago, the tubes filled nostrils and sometimes anuses, but these proved too moist and, indeed, were often occupied already. The ear, on the other hand, was so hospitable that it doubled the survival rate of the offspring and seemed as well to yield happier tubes, if rambunctiousness and curvature are any indication.

As one would imagine, the tubes must be attached to a spigot of some kind for anything to flow out of them. Enter the female. She molds her opening around a tube and blows her eggs through it, where they are mixed with his foam before squirting out the other end.

The ears remain a mystery. Though they are now cultivated for the purpose, it is believed they were once live game, attached to people's heads.

As a wedding gift, a set of ears is customarily given to bride and groom in hopes they will be filled that very night.

Yet, a certain species of prairie wolf has taken to licking out the ears, something it would never have done to the anuses.

The Switch

"Why do you dwell in this pond?" came the daylight query.

I answered thus: "In this pond is my oil."

"Cannot you keep your oil within?"

"It is not that kind of oil," I said with embarrassment. Such a response never failed to perplex them.

"Cannot you keep your oil without?" one ventured after a moment.

"Precisely!" said I with a show of enthusiasm that crossed his eyes, not that I could be sure of the sex.

"Tell us about this sex," said another, evidently proud to have picked my mind. I ratcheted up my defenses.

"Why do you suppose I'm soaking in this pond?" I asked and then had to answer for them: "Fish eggs!"

"Fisheggs?" they said, running the words together.

"This place is crawling with them."

"And they… produce the oil?" they asked.

"Precisely!"

"Your oil?"

"That's what they tell me."

Meanwhile, I had managed to locate the switch. It was hidden beneath the muck at the bottom of the pond. With my big toe, I flipped it off and was plunged head first into the place they couldn't reach me. At least not until morning.

Maude

Having grown herself up from a speck, Maude (the name given her by those who'd overseen the growth) decided it was time to go out in the world and act. And the principal action she could think to perform was to attract another to her who'd grown up from a speck at about the same time and in about the same place, so that they might together provide for the growth of other specks that came first out of his body and then out of hers.

In the land where they were born, however, there was a ritual to observe, a ritual handed down from grown speck to grown speck, though none were aware any longer of its original meaning or purpose. The observance kept Maude from performing effectively what she presumed to be her principal action.

The ritual was this: One must strip bare all Soil Suckers (trees) within thirty feet of one's domicile. This included the needles or leaves, of course, but also branches and twigs. As they lived in a forest and had none of our modern tools, performing this ritual was often a life-long endeavor. Sure, most were able to stop a few years before death but by then they had no idea what else to do with themselves, so they hung around other people's Soil Suckers, giving advice.

Because of this, Maude had little time or energy to find and attract a proper mate and ended up with a speck from near the great boulder, whose parents were unmistakable models for what her future held. It was all laid out before her now. The stripped trees, the baby specks, the brief getaways to neighboring forests, the health problems, the near completing of the ritual only to move and have to start from scratch, the completing of it at last only to realize you've long ago forgotten what else to do with yourself, the stiff naked poles surrounding you like stakes…

Instructions

When you open your holes to breathe, they pour in. When you lift your eyelids to see, they smother your vision into kaleidoscopic hallucinations. They're already in your ears, making you hear things you've never imagined, something akin, perhaps, to whales' songs crammed like sardines into transistor radios. Out come your instructions. Impossible to decipher, yet easy enough to intuit into some sort of action, usually involving the growth of more tissue for their young to feed on. The kind of tissue growth required does not happen automatically in the body, like the growth of a lung, but only from the coaxing of such seemingly garbled instructions. Most of the time, you don't even know it's happening, which must be for the best.

I remember once a sea of green, a green of such mesmerizing beauty that I failed to notice it coming further onto the shore with each pulse. Naturally, I assumed the pulses were ocean waves, though the crashing sounds had dissolved in favor of a mounting atonal humming that, like the green of the sea, held me spellbound. I'm not sure I ever left that shore. We could be there still, hidden beneath the waves.

Daniel Grandbois is the author of *Unlucky Lucky Days* and *The Hermaphrodite: An Hallucinated Memoir*. Also a musician, he plays in three of the pioneering bands of "The Denver Sound": Slim Cessna's Auto Club, Tarantella, and Munly.

Lightning

I chomp at the black, bats everywhere. I drag you to a little room to show you 116 photos, six orange ones of big mushroom clouds. *You are lucky you made it* you say straight into my eyes. I flail my arms and make a gesture *like the water is always flipping.* So you bring out the urn.

I capsize the urn and cover myself in a soot suit, feel something ugly disappear, then scream when a handprint appears on the hip.

Sometimes I hope for new blood while trying to start my birthday. Any suit of yours I slip into is a nice birthday.

I emerge from the little room and climb aboard a tractor then get off the tractor to board a boat in the middle of a long bleak storm. That was days ago. It is nice here now. I've been missing you though you mailed a bag of money. I spend a handful when I'm sad. Days ago on the road the weather crushed down and crushed the tulips and muddied the soot. Now the weather is a big blue man and I am a muddy small woman. The first thing I see from the water is a seventies-ish rainbow. It is a little strange, deceitful, and I climb the mountain with nowhere to go.

Girls on the Run

I am what I remember. I am a life whose heart was so close it tongued you when you were old enough to live within the two hours and old enough to see 25 kinds of what exists within the dunes. I remember the last fisherpeople left coconut milk to swarm with crabs; blue on the moonlit dunes, blue on the small island of huts. Around the crabs swarmed 13 children, boys, and those boys I remember made a landscape of handholds below where one airplane a week would fly over.

I remember the skin you were old enough to shock and lightning so rich the corncobs still in their husks popped. I remember the dunes. To celebrate in an ungoverned realm the bees must live in harmony with the snake-seekers someone said. A woman covered the girls' arms in bat blood so they wouldn't grow hair there. To unearth a pink bike rolling past, you must slip a fish into the moonlight someone said. Where we lie now in two hours will swarm with 13 children, boys, and all will slip their imaginations toward the girls peeking from the green hill, bat-blood arms frailly flailing like bat wings. In an ungoverned land a slick and subtle shock brings lightning cut from the next monsters.

One uncle says the way to become a beautiful firefly is to celebrate the parrots, even, to offer their green feathers, beaks, acorn-sized hearts—and everything else they have—cut out, cut open, and itemized, to the beast family. Later in the shed he shucks off his jeans down to the skin as a present and there his penis hangs like a melted elephant nose.

To be on the run is to be a week overgrown with green, green hills, a gift of emeralds rolling from one end of the cradle to the other, to mimic the flight pattern of an animal with no ears. Offer your green and subtle shock to the core before you throw the lightning into the pot. Only one airplane a week lands on this island, and it is a sick surge aliens feel when they discover skin made for men's pleasure sucks clouds out of the air.

The family, the core opening up before you from the beasts I remember faintly. The moonlight. What we could withstand was cut from the ceiling and those born into it were bound and cut and tagged and branded and their baby teeth saved for spells. An uncle cascades in with a carved whistle as a present and later shucks his jeans off in a violent rip.

We lie, and we lie, and we lie, and after two hours I have 25 kinds of sex with you right on this island. It is like this island is ruled by sickness mined from the bottom of the core and it is ours too. I remember to make the children safe. This I remember. I was a life whose heart was rich and later it tongued you through the ceiling.

SUMMARY OF A MOON FILM

When the front door opens there are some broken off pieces of man there on the welcome mat. She is awful to accept such deliveries. She once loved the man and never touched him, they just played tug-o-war with a long piece of silk.

I watch her in an alley. She is so alien, like a prostitute. She picks up her own hellish, claustrophobic isolation and throws it. I watch an important messenger tell her something.

She is unaware of the little bits of fabric he would sew into her palms: in private she squelches her poise and it is awful to hear silence exist in such a perfect American accent.

He carries silks and batiks on his way. She is in love with someone she can't open her pain in front of. She has spoken only once in her life, and it was a long time ago, and it was about a city full of rivers. In public her desire is so painfully fraught that it crumbles down. In private she can't open her mouth.

Between two hours lies the rest of the woman. This moment, at the end, of course, is when she tries to eat rice. She picks up a little picture of a city, elegantly spare. There is a world between the viewer and her mouth.

This moment will not crumble down her chin.

The servant sews words into his tongue and stays in the same two alleys witnessing this painful exchange from a payphone. O her elegant robes, O her elegant robes.

Her master wafts by and no one speaks. They walk in and out of the same two rooms, holding the silk. At the end she can't perform her duties and carries a basket of rice to the city, speaking in English about the rivers there. There is a prostitute in the audience who can't locate her throat.

Blue Kill

I had a dream that he killed the sun by bloodletting the ram, by draining its heat. Sitting there to the left was the day. Staring at him was a sleeping woman and a knife.

My friend quit alcohol 16 years ago after drinking six liters of himself. He stared at himself. Two hours later his eyes made a flood. They broke most of the mirror, looked at a mountaintop and never woke up. He barely knew who said *he barely knew the man.* He killed the middle of the mirror after a sleeping woman who lay facedown on his right handed him the knife. He sat straight up and saw his own ghost. My friend spent most of the night bloodletting the bed. He looked into the ram's eye, drained its blood and looked to his right. He walked downstairs to another sleeping woman. The ram also looked into his eyes with big brown eyes. They spent most of the day staring at each other, then his wife called, hysterical, and screamed that he was dying.

My friend walked through the middle of vodka by himself until he found the knife, then looked into the mirror at a sweaty, blue-white, translucent version of the ram. Its blood flowed all over hotel room 201. After waking up in the day to stare at it, his wife called. Two hours later a man he barely knew said she had had a mountaintop-dream that he was dying. He stared. Two hours later his eyes flooded. A man he barely knew drove him to find help. The man was a sweaty, blue-white, translucent version of night.

Julie Doxsee is the author of two books, *Undersleep* (Octopus Books 2008) and *Objects for a Fog Death* (Black Ocean 2009). She lives in Istanbul, Turkey.

He sits, is sitting, can't move from in front of the console. Jitter is the word, jitter, jitter. Nervous? No. Zaps of what to do impale him, a blimp in paralysis. No script for the hunger he's having. He's a big body, see those fingers over the keys? And humility, how those fingers bend. How, writing, this will get it wrong, except for the hunger.

The blue sky square over the monitor could be another screen and there's a pool you pay to float below in it. Start again says those blues, you've done it. But every blue effort expires.

Eating is the least of it. He eats for two, she eats for four, that's six on a die-et. Rice is the least of it.

Parents are trickling toward him, they're too old and he's at an age and stopped, there, under his fingers, in front of the console.

Because you get brown hair, that's why. In a parking space that no matter how backward, you can't pull into it. Or out. The traffic behind you makes a terrible racket, you have to pee. And you still have brown hair.

She hands you a nice hot cup of water. Nice to blow on. She still has her heft but part of her forearm, her back arm, flaps, in old lady flaps where the fat has fled in surprise so fast. Her silence stares, she let the cat go the day before, walked it as far as she could, given the size of her still, and at once it prowled, turned back. But only once. They're not like dogs, she says after she shuts the window screen tight. They see promise of scraps and that's all there is to it—loyalty.

The snake they ate. He made a sly hole in the cage she couldn't imagine useful, and it exited onto the pan. She didn't ask how the rice had bone. Meat was hardly involved.

One tank of gas left for where? Emergencies do not unfold despite his fingers poised, they are bold and transgress. He won't answer the phone. He has never met whoever lives around them in their complex, not even their 6A opposites, it is that complex, their quiet. They take the apartment only for the pool, its reflection of that final blue. Drugless, they want that drug.

Now he can't flee the console. Sex lies mournful on his thigh near enough to her lying in a corpse-pose, corpulent. He admires her body with the mindless need of the gluttonous, with nothing less about it. He admires and still he sits, his mind working its hunger without him. Earlier, he told his parents from his bed, his sole console support, he told them that he is fully employed but deep in the night so whenever they call in the day he can say he is asleep. They lead with their questions on their messages, he thinks up lies as answers, the silence between keeping it cordial. Because his answer will be a broken leg between them, something forced, the leg exchanged and handed back and forth, its bloody arteries spewing, but still given and taken, they call anyway often.

His happiness doesn't answer. He's a t-shirt in a Sim family, a hairshirt someone has to scratch. His fingers move over the keys as if a piano's, his instrument, his Zombie explosion, his Save or not, its Help menu. He kills and kills while he lies, his happiness fully invested in electricity. This time their message says *Come home.* His fingers can't fire fast enough.

When she reports from wherever she poses her corpse, prone with the day's discouragement, *Too many tattoos!* or *They can't make the aisles wider*, he tells her a story about Sigmund Freud, how sometimes a cigar is a cigar.

She wasn't chosen to know the latest, she says. She knows about cigars.

He kisses her knuckle with tenderness, light with his lips still puckered after. He harbors many wishes, they bubble up and join the blue in a paroxysm like held breath. He is blue with wishes that escape. Then rain.

TERESE SVOBODA'S *Trailer Girl and Other Stories* is being reissued in paper this fall. Her fifth and sixth novels are due out 2010 and 2011.

Blown Exits

Often I mistake that I am pregnant. I go dizzy, rung with size. My skin will swim with liquid. Double heartbeat. Rhythmic blood.

Some cold evenings in this reeling, someone's in me. Someone numb or wanting. Someone there.

Soon I will come across my name.

There was a name once, this I'm sure of, though all my papers, prizes, lockets have gone black or blank.

It's been some time since I enjoyed a celebration or felt the blood run through my hands.

The stretch marks down my forearms match the wood grain of the room beneath my room, though sometimes that room is made of mud. Sometimes there isn't any room at all.

There are often words I can convince myself I've gone by till I remember what each word means.

One month I sloshed around calling myself DEERHEAD till I hit one with my car and both the deer and car were killed.

I'd convinced myself my name was HOLE till I fell down one—between the wall where all the flies sit and the sofa where I sit up when I can't sleep. I fell for quite some time—and sometimes feel still falling—the air rushed in my lungs.

Other names that I have gone by: BABY, BATHROOM, WINDPIPE, SLUGGER, BOB or BOBBY, NEON, BOOK.

Here in the evenings I feel small. This flesh is kind of crushing.

(I know there's not really someone else.)

I had a wig I liked to wear once but it started going gray.

The mites mired in my back skin skew the sensors in my tongue. I bite an apple, tastes like Corn Flakes. I lick a new wound—buttermilk.

My saliva by itself is spicy.

My throat is always sore.

I'm not sure who keeps painting my den walls darker colors. It started crème and shifted down a shade each week. After black came something else, where if you stood and scrunched yourself a certain way, there was no one in the room.

I tend to agree with everything that's mentioned.

I would give you this whole house.

When I get in bed I lash my legs around to make sure of no one else.

Sometimes I'll find a large scab or strand of hair meshed into the sheets where through nights I've sweated all my water in this endless cycle. Always so much noise stuffed in my pillow, no matter which ear, or how hot or cold, etc.

I don't know what I have a bed for—I sleep better on the ground, with my head close to the spinning.

Sometimes the spinning is like free TV.

Other times I wish I knew how to remove my whole head. That's not meant to sound morbid, mostly—any more than any spoken thing will surely be.

Whatever my name was, my father called me something different, though I can't remember that either, at all.

My father used to knock with just one knuckle so we could tell for sure it was him—though surely anyone could do the same.

My father, in his dawning, often liked to hear himself make sound. In the hall outside my bed at night he'd stand against the wall and yarble. He'd coocoo like a rubber ducky, peering through me. His fingers had deep ridges. As time went on, the ridges deepened with his cancer.

I'll respond to mostly any form of address, even HEY YOU, even GOD.

I've found my blood has different flavors depending on how and where it's drawn.

I didn't brush my teeth for years.

One week for several evenings I was stuck and could not move. Each time I could move again I tried to not.

Each time I try to not is when I can.

Depending on where I stop along the hallway, in this long house, I hear different kinds of sound.

I remember people singing sometime.

I'm not sure what there is to sing about.

I can always find at least one fingerprint left on a mirror, even right out of the box.

There was someone who used the guest bathroom more than a few times for shaving but they always took care to rinse the sink.

There are certain books that I can't look in without feeling someone's there over my shoulder.

The wood floor in the kitchen sometimes changes grain.

My bed is big enough for several people but most nights it's just me.

I say *most*, I mean *every single one entirely without question.*

Sometimes I'll realize I've been talking aloud for some time and have no idea just what's been said, or who the talking could have been to, or who could hear.

I'm pretty sure I'm colorblind, though for different colors than other people are. Like when I look into the backyard sometimes all I see is white.

Certain books I've read before I'll reopen and see the text is all just gone.

Used to be, anytime I needed another person all I'd have to do is order pizza.

Again, OK, here just now, someone behind me in the room…

I swear I am not getting any older, no matter how I try.

I'll hear one long slow tone in one ear for weeks or hours, then just nothing, then the other ear.

I played a tuba for like eighteen years until one day I just gave up.

Sometimes I pretend that I am playing it using my water belly for the bulb. I use the nodules on my forearms for buttons.

The nodules, they are cysts, I'm pretty sure. They seem sometimes to shift locations. The strain will firm against my hands.

I am again feeling very tired.

I don't know who would have made an earth from all this dirt.

BLAKE BUTLER morvsosiss lak bahd lordbeedumbandis osklunt. Bishtoklet inkvar moyn inisis isit perdormidordidum-unk, lob budditt kroidbullellerreruminnitigben boiby bo.

On Water and the City

I

Unlike everything else, water ascends as easily as it descends—it appears in puddles on the floor and, having come from an unknown source, is oddly inspirational. If a wise man was to appear, he might say, "be of the ways of water—appear and disappear, be originless and always ready to change form."

The humidity of a place is revealed in the condition of its paint. Excessive humidity, for example, is visible if the paint peels and curls, revealing 1) dry, sinewy wood underneath its surface, and 2) raised edges that are best described as "serrated," "labial," or "crystalline."

Other clues: texture, mutability, immutability, gauze, gray areas and intermediate states, mist, fog, steam, surface giving way to surface, inside succumbing to outside, color becoming place-specific, time-specific, dependent upon the various charcoals of the sky…

Decay and wear are the results of specific processes and intensities in which—with the passing of time—buildings become charming, people become detestable, questions become philosophical, water becomes stagnant (fertile), the subjects of fermentation ferment, the decomposing decompose, and the soon to be digested are digested.

Appearances, thus, do not betray "age," but rather, "what has been endured."

II

Evaporation, fermentation, and composture are voluntary transformations in which individuals cultivate plural and unnamable states.

An individual who clutches onto ideal images of the world and his/herself is best as a rock formation or plaster—the word "vestigial," for example, signifies both impressive buildings and reactionary, intolerable men.

To say that [x] building is "worn" is to say that [x] is *actively asking questions of* and *making allusions to* its present and past states. If we are, for example, to be in a place where [y] catastrophe has occurred, it is difficult to look at any worn [x] and not immediately attribute all visible damage and wear to [y]—the flaw in this thinking is, of course, the variable [z] which, signifying *everything aside from [y]*, is much more likely the cause.

It is also through [z] that one learns of the often exploitative nature of unbridled, associative thinking and, more generally, of attraction.

The shared meanings of water and milk, both literal and symbolic, are false. Although milk is a liquid, it does not flood, erode, or necessitate aqueducts.

Digging, I find water. I feel bound to a minor, ignorant reality (abundance of water). Rain continues to fill these gaps.

III

I am wearing a veil that, although it has an interior space inside of which I always reside (it is not the kind of veil one can easily remove), is defined by what lies outside of it.

More: my outside is outside of the outside of this place—it is outside of these streets and parks; outside of the inside of these buildings. My veil is invisible but, somehow, the locals immediately sense it and, surrounding me, they ask questions: is it (the veil) penetrable? is it hot? is it a lens and, if it is, of what strength is it? is it sad to know that one's own world-view is so perpetually distorted?

There are certain areas of this city that lend easily to daydreaming and other kinds of 'idle' and 'narcotic' thinking. This experience, however, is not entirely communicable as its truth is not exterior to my veil, but, I want to ask them in return, *what is?*

As an adolescent, I was most satisfied when riding the ferry from my home city to a nearby island and thus, when I was given the freedom to do so, I rode the ferry as much as I could, often for hours at a time, unable to free myself from the cycle of endless arrival and return until the ferry had closed for the day.

A sense of sleepiness is so pervasive here that, nearly everywhere, one finds droves of people either sitting or slowly milling about—like clouds, they loiter on balconies and curbs; talking, reading, crowding the cafes and bars, playing cards, and occasionally resting a skeptical eye upon me or one of the other thousand tourists who, keeping our heads to ground, want nothing more than the impossible, sudden *something* (opportunity/affair/inspiration/invitation)—the moment in which the city offers more than we have known in other places.

IV

The "sensations," "feelings," and "experiences" specific to a place are airborne and—like pollen, dust, and other particles—they inspire a host of reactions in the people who ingest them. Although it is fair to call them "toxins" in the sense that they intoxicate, they are not to be considered "carcinogens" or "physically harmful" in any way.

The pleasure I take in crossing the small drawbridges that span the canals of this city is, similar to my experiences with the ferry, rooted in waiting and the observations afforded by situations in which one waits among a group of people who share no connections beyond their waiting.

At night, however, there is nothing but exposure in the overall lack of light; the static (odd pleasure) of vulnerability.

A field, if left silent and idle, will fall to the decentralized rule of weeds, rodents, insects, and other wild plants—this is also the case with minds and zoneless, unmonitored cities like this one.

Digging, I realize that—although I have always found water when digging—it is not axiomatic to find water when digging. To say that my being is "tautological" is, perhaps, a resignation to my naïveté and the overall narrowness of my mind and experience.

V or 'brief address to a generalized *you*'

These are the last moments in which you will be here. There is someplace you must go and I too, to a place where I must go. Possibilities are like cities: we either walk through them or imagine ourselves walking through them. We consider that departure is *necessary* and *inevitable*. We consider that, in order to maintain self-interest, there must be a method better than this constant combining and re-combining of things.

Anxiety and self-consciousness are, it seems, sieve-shaped: one can use a pestle to work as much liquid as possible out of the fleshy, raspberry mass, but some useless by-product (tendency) always remains.

When washing one's own hands it is not uncommon to leave small puddles or droplets on the floor. The nature of [hands] is imperfection although [hands] are perfect in form.

To allow the flawless, beautiful way in which an individual washes his or her hands imply to a higher, absolute perfection of that individual, is to see a false image.

VI or 'encounter with resident K'

K: The feeing is that of being (in) a box. It is to admit to slowness, distance, and the idea that forward is adrift and that this certain conception of adrift is best described by the state of being inside of or otherwise assuming the form of a box.

Me: Ahhh, you are speaking of the imaginary network – proof that the nature of the unexpected is unexpected, that the tendency to describe certain phenomena as without reason or random is, in actuality, NOT an indication of "ignorance" or "an inability to count enough moves ahead as to comprehend the complexity of the game."

K: No, not exactly.

OR

K: I prefer you silent. To call your speech 'figurative' is flattery – 'narcissistic' or 'masturbatory,' it seems, would be more appropriate.

OR

K: Your interpretation of my statement is highly flawed and, not to mention, highly offensive to anyone with even a basic knowledge of psychoanalysis.

OR

K: If you decide to stay inside the box for eternity, I would think, yes.

VII

Although all places have at least one unique thing about them, the world is, ultimately, unfair. There is a hierarchy of interesting places in which qualities like *not destroyed by [x] war* and *at the cultural center of [y] people* are of the highest value. Places, like people, are born into situations beyond their control and, although one place can pity another and feel guilty for its own prosperity, it will learn—as everyone learns—of the convenience of insularity.

It is upon a long road of water that one comes to this place—the sensation is either that of teetering-over something (preparing to drop) or, otherwise, of sitting cross-legged upon the concrete bed of an empty lock (waiting to be filled)—"fairness," I said "is a foreboding thing. There is always the possibility that everything and everybody will be caught up with and justice, eventually, executed." K, surprised by the lateness of my reply, scoffs at me and, eventually, walks away.

"The feeling," I say to myself, "is that of embarrassment; of watching a loved-one wince and recoil at my advancing."

VIII or 'uncertain analysis'

The depopulation suffered here is so severe that one not only finds abandoned, sunken buildings among inhabited structures, but there are also entire "ghost" blocks and neighborhoods embedded within the city. Water, I want to say, is responsible for all of this as the brown, sandy line of its former level can be seen upon so many of the victims' façades.

Buildings are more prone to death in places that have been emptied out (the experience of being totally abandoned)—a great deal is lost when transferring (substances, water, people) between containers.

And: it seems that people, who are also dying, are best accompanied by dying buildings.

My uncertainty, however, is the kind of uncertainty that is compulsory to foreigners. It is to say, with every word I speak, "I fear I have said too much."

IX or 'the inhuman successor of K'

We could have kept at it. We could have snuck off to an attic or a basement and been among objects whose stories have, like our own, fallen out with time—we could have clumsily bumped around those objects, trying to tell our own stories, failing in the company of the failed, collecting dust in the company of the dusty, but we didn't, we decided not to; we parted.

To say that I imagine you have eyes in such and such a way would be to say that I imagine you have eyes. It would be to say that an eye is not an eye (in terms of the visual cycle) and that the entire world and the atmosphere are eyes.

Supposedly, there exists a liquid that lubricates the eyes better than water. We have been told that such a chemical has been produced and, presently, is under observation by a panel of officials who may or may not approve the drug for public use. I was told this liquid is special because it is water-based yet insoluble in water and, astoundingly, it never dries-up. Such a liquid, I was told, would eliminate the need for natural tears, whose purpose it is to lubricate the eyes.

X

My socks, my pants, my groin, my back, my pants, my backpack, my notebooks, my wallet, my sweater and shirt: all of them wet.

What remains is what we arrive upon (always). Museums of evidence are not only to be found in predictably hidden places, but also in the streets and public domains of the city. The visible cross-sections of buildings and soil, for example, reveal a certain logic of the city that can only be discovered by means of repeated, careful observation.

The city's story is free from the demystified state into which history and other documents have rendered it. The story is occult, vague, and spoken by a single subject (the city) with several voices (its residents, past and present), all of them speaking simultaneously. It is like the taking-off of several birds in several directions—in order to understand, one must follow the birds.

One can, for example, discover the topography of this place through the fluctuations in height of water-marks that are visible on girders and other structures throughout the city.

Water, like the city, has its own memory, a quality observable in the similarity of the concentric rings that form whenever an object breaks its surface.

XI

My mistake was in attempting to hold you to a word and, moreover, in my attempting to hold that word to a single image or shadow of itself. I did these things for the purpose of convenience and, binding you to the word and the meaning-systems of words, I objectified you—I re-discovered you as a tool; as something I could, depending upon the situation, either excite or scare myself with.

As a body, I have learned, you are false—your images, your signals, your signs—all of them false.

Although I have long been told to avoid misrepresentations of all kinds, it has always been the case that I become most excited when discovering the ways in which a place connives; in learning the ways in which I can expose myself to the dangers of a place while reserving a possibility for escape.

There is also, however, the ability reserved by a place to bestow upon an individual a series of so-called "phantasmagorically horrifying" images and/or events.

I have, thus, concerning my visits to unfamiliar neighborhoods, have set the following limits: only during daytime, by bicycle, and wearing tattered, loose linen in order to appear as if a monk or somehow depossessed of the world.

XII

If you are to be a body and, if such a body is to move, you are to seduce. If you are to be connectivity, you are to be fog or otherwise the chemicals (neurotransmitters) found in and around synapses. If you are to be yourself—a city—I am to consider you from a high place where I can see your lackings laid-bare.

Eventually one realizes that, in this city, everyone is walking around with gauze wrapped around their faces; everything they see is as I see it: through sheets and sheets and sheets and sheets of water.

Today, I will say goodbye and I will turn around afterwards and then around again, saying goodbye once more. I will commence to repeatedly walk in and out of a closet, sometimes coming out with hangers or moth-balls stuck to me, but no matter what my condition is when exiting the closet, I will quickly retreat into the darkness, closing the door behind me, exiting, and repeating the process until I arrive home.

It seems it would be easier to imagine a desertic world; a place where—due to the great shortage of water—one is certain as to both why and for what reason he or she lives. In abundance, water seems sinister and even mocking at times, only suggesting that things will continue on in this way—this constant, slow waiting.

STEPHEN GROPP-HESS lives in Tuscaloosa, Alabama. He is, among other things, obsessed with texts and manifestos of fragmentation.

according to tradition we are to lift the weight of the funeral off our house with the use of some thin linen, lace or silk. these funeral rags, before being hung from the four, or however many corners of the courtyard, must be soaked for at least half a day in the gray water collected from a communal bath, attended by all relatives younger than the deceased, held in the largest possible trough in the village. during this time, the body, if present, must be coated, by the mother when alive, when not, an older sister, if no sister is alive, then by the oldest mother of the village whose first son is alive, with enough mud and lime to be left to dry in sun or moon. this is to avoid the smell and the nostalgia emanating from the body thickening the air we breathe and the air that settles on our skin. there simply is no tolerance for that. if the body is not present, and as long as the family does not demand otherwise, the empty coffin, wrapped in thick wool blankets, will be taken away by volunteers to the coffin house, where it will be saved for those who, like the ones born with physical disabilities, in their lifetime did not get a chance to dig for their own empty coffin,[1] but the coffin object[2] is left to the family.

it is the mothers' task to tie the rags together while they are still wet. as long as strong, their knots are free to express their grief, the tightening of their mourning. the two youngest fathers of the family are assigned to climb to the roof and hang the material from the hooks affixed to the corners of the courtyard by fathers from earlier generations. after they hang the rags and stretch them across the courtyard, it is the youngest walking daughter's duty to gather, for the garlic fire, as many heads of garlic as the deceased's age. she is to pick, if in season from the garden, and if not, from the village pantry with an appropriate order slip. tradition states that the heads of garlic be burned one by one until

---

[1] *empty coffin.* most excavated empty coffins are actually not empty but contain the remains of the previous coffin object. the excavator holds the right to either keep or destroy these remains. see "a complete list of things to do before dying."

[2] *coffin object.* it is every individual's duty to choose a coffin object that will be put inside their empty coffin instead of themselves. a record of this object is kept in the individual's confidential folder at the elders council's archives. a coffin object, once chosen and registered, unless death intervenes, cannot be changed. in the past there have been those who chose their spouses, children, goats, wolves etc. as their coffin object and tradition was carried out without exception.

the material hanging in the courtyard turns yellow. if there is a blind member of the family, and as long as his or her age permits, the garlic fire is his or her duty, if not, the elders council assigns to it a blind villager, experienced in burning the garlic.

with every funeral the first thing to be replaced is the door to the courtyard of the deceased's family. it is forbidden that the funeral procession leave the courtyard before the door is replaced. for the new door, three members of the family are to climb up to the plateau and fell a big walnut tree at least nine branches old. this task requires raw, big-blood bravery, because the dervishes dominating the plateaus are of a cruel breed who regard the walnut a sacred fruit. so, to avoid the wrath of the dervishes, those climbing the plateau must coincide their climb with the dervishes' communal prayer hours held on the eastern slopes. but, since the dervishes count time using a method still unknown to us, this timing is often miscalculated and often it is that the walnut in the plateau causes yet another funeral. still, we understand, more clearly at such times, that tradition, is not some force that allows yesterday into today, but on the contrary, a sort of bridge that weaves today into the days ahead, like an old table game, preparing us to live to the possibilities of tomorrows.

those successful in felling the walnut and bringing it to the village are given the right to carry around their necks the key to the new door of that courtyard. after enough board square is milled and used for the new door, it is the head carpenter's duty to carve out a receptacle for the deceased's ashes. the head carpenter is supposed to seal this receptacle with the help of some pitch-mortar and send it to the village kiln to be flash-fired. from the kiln the receptacle is delivered to the volunteer firefighters in charge of cremation.

as the garlic fire ceases, it is again the mothers' responsibility to untie the rags and, after setting aside enough of them to wrap the coffin object, hang them, unlike at a wedding, on the outside of the house windows, as curtains. it is the oldest member of the family who, after being informed by the elders council, finds and wraps the coffin object to be placed inside the empty coffin. meanwhile the village barber washes the body from the mud and lime, shaves and burns all its hair, removes all its teeth and strings the ones that are in good condition for further storage. the body is then placed on a rosewood and wicker stretcher and carried on the shoulders of the volunteer firefighters to the highest point of the village where it is burnt with the fire-head pointing against the wind. the remains that do not get carried away by the wind are put inside the receptacle and taken directly to the dock, to the sea-room. here, the receptacle is chained by the head spear-man, locked with the old lock of the courtyard door and taken out to sea on the black boat. the boatman to row the black boat out to sea is chosen by the funeral family only if the deceased is believed to have died of a holy cause. if it is not known how and why the deceased has died or if he or she has died of natural causes, a boatman unknown to the family is assigned by the sea-room for the job. the boatman is to row his black oars until the big white anchor hanging on the sea-room becomes invisible and as much as the sea allows him, forget where he throws the receptacle into the water.

when the sound of the cannon fired from the sea-room at the black boat's return echoes from those waters we have not dared to go for so long now, the new door to the courtyard must be hung on its hinges so the procession can make its way out. the order of the procession according to the old tradition[3] is as follows: the elders council at the head, then the coffinmen with the empty coffin, then the enemies, the neighbors, the acquaintances, and the family of the deceased, then the rest of the village folk, followed by the shepherds chorus. as the procession reaches the monument-rock[4] through a route designated by the elders council, both the shepherds' pipes and the rattles must come to silence, for this is the time for weeping, and those who are going to cry after the dead must save themselves until this time. if the deceased

---

[3] *old tradition procession.* in the past some elders requested the exclusion of the shepherds chorus' requiems from the choreography of the funeral procession. these requiems, played by the shepherds on their buxus wood pipes, had a profound effect of grief on the villagers who not only were unable to carry out their duties but also disrupted the course of the procession. this resulted in the introduction of the wooden rattles. when used by all attendees of the funeral, the sound of the rattles drown the requiems of the shepherds chorus and prevents misconduct. although still in effect, after a short period of time the elders council excused themselves of the rattle.

[4] *monument-rock.* what tradition tells us is that our ancestors, before building their village, wanted to establish a central point, a center of gravity. they marked that point with the biggest rock in the area that could be carried by mortal strength. we are not sure as to the originality of this point but our calculations and planning today keep the monument-rock in the center of our village. generations in the past have tried moving, carving, giving the monument-rock a form other than its raw form, but over time they learned that the composition of the rock does not allow sculpting, that it is surprisingly deep-rooted and heavy.

has died in daylight, the circumambulation of the monument-rock is done clockwise, and if the deceased has died in the dark, or if the time of death is not known, the circumambulation is done counter-clockwise.

all are free to circumambulate the monument-rock after the necessary turns have been completed, but the coffinmen must put down the coffin at the base of the monument-rock. those who are not willing to walk more gather into a tight circle around the monument-rock to hear the whispering elegies of the elders council members. the elders choose the elegies they will recite either according to how the deceased has died or how the deceased was known in the village. these elegies, that the elders study soundlessly under their mustaches during their walk, are stories of how our ancestors touched death itself, how they walked hand in hand with it, how they escaped it, how they died with it and how they couldn't die at all. as these stories culture and become yogurt in the elders' mouths, the rest of the procession stop their circumambulation and join the circle. most people throw handfuls of paint on the monument-rock and try to mark the date but no paint lasts long enough, all fade and are forgotten. the funeral is dismissed after the last elegy is put out. the family of the deceased close the door to the courtyard from the inside and engage in a verbal fast for a day, at the end of which the oldest member, again, to break the fast, opens his mouth and gives sound to the deceased's name for the last time.

the night of the funeral, the empty coffin left at the base of the monument-rock is taken and buried in a random location by an unknown entity. for generations the village folk has kept watch on funeral nights and witnessed the coffin disappear before their eyes. today some believe it to be the works of our ancestors, some suggest the dervishes and everyone awaits an answer. but as it writes in every council book, "there is no one answer, and therefore there is no one question. there are only questions."

—translated from Turkish by the author

Ali Aktan Aşkın's writings have previously appeared in ***Sleepingfish*** and ***elimae***. He is currently relocating from the West coast of Turkey to rural Maine, where he will try to keep the wood stove burning.